ROYAL MARINE
COMMANDO

ROYAL MARINE
COMMANDO

JAMES D LADD

Foreword by
Lieutenant General Sir Steuart R Pringle, Bt
Commandant General of the Royal Marines

HAMLYN
London · New York · Sydney · Toronto

Overleaf: A Mountain
Leader (ML) climbs a snow
slope. MLs are trained
specialists in Mountain and
Arctic Warfare (M & AW)
and serve in reconnaissance
troops as well as training
the Corps' instructors in
mountaineering.

First published 1982
Second impression 1982
Third impression 1983

© James D Ladd 1982

Published by
The Hamlyn Publishing Group Limited
London · New York · Sydney · Toronto
Astronaut House, Feltham, Middlesex, England

ISBN 0 600 34203 4
Printed in Italy

Contents

Foreword

In his last two books, *Commandos and Rangers of World War II* and *Royal Marines 1919–80*, James Ladd has written extensively about the Royal Marines in this century. Now, in *Royal Marine Commando*, he looks back over three centuries of what Sir Winston Churchill described as rough tough history in a search for the origins of the qualities displayed by Royal Marines today.

One volume is too small a vehicle for any history of the Marines but what Mr Ladd, himself a former Royal Marines officer, has written is a pastiche of events great and small, battles and skirmishes, the strategy of campaigns and the heroism of individual men. Each element of his story provides an ingredient, a flavour or a savouring for the whole and the whole is garnished with photographs, many of which have never been published before.

What the individual reader gains is between himself and the author, but at the conclusion of this very readable volume you cannot fail to understand better why His Royal Highness Prince Philip, our Captain General, was able to say with confidence, 'A Royal Marine Commando is always expected to achieve the impossible.'

Lieutenant General
Sir Steuart R Pringle, Bt

Preface

The exciting history of raids, amphibious assault and of war by land and sea, is the heritage of the Royal Marines. To this they link in the 1980s the commando heritage, stemming from the American Rangers fighting for the British in 1755, the Boers' self-reliance and the stirring actions of the British army commandos of the 1940s. In such a long tradition there are many actions, assault landings and inventive tactics, of which only examples can be given in depth. However in the notes with each chapter are brief summaries of all the major actions in which Royal Marines took part and other points of detail.

The Royal Marines' history encompassed also a tradition of naval gunnery, one of their principal roles from the 1830s until the early 1950s. This service, although not directly related to commando techniques of the 1980s, has its place in the origins of the commandos' versatility – as indeed does the Marines' early roles in fitting out ships – for a commando is above all a man of many abilities. A sharp mind as much as supreme physical fitness, self-reliance and personal discipline, are his characteristics in the Royal Marine tradition, as is apparent from this history. While his ability to carry through operations with an individual determination might be said to be his commando heritage, as one of a superb force of light infantryman in the twentieth century.

The records of Marine history before 1755 are incomplete; and some conjecture has inevitably been necessary therefore over the early actions described in the text. But a detailed list of sources are held by the author, limitations of space preventing their inclusion in the book. The dates recorded are those of contemporary documents but before 1752 these differed from the modern calendar by up to eleven days. There are summarized details of organisation in the Appendices.

I am most grateful to General Sir Steuart Pringle Bt for his foreword, and for the help of Major A J Donald RM the Corps Historical Records Officer. My thanks also for their assistance in researching details for the book are acknowledged to the Museum staff and in particular: their Director, Maj A G Brown MBE RM; the Curator, Mr Paul Fauset; the Archivist, Miss Bridget Spiers; the Keeper of the Photographic Library, Mr Harry Playford; and the Librarian Mr Matthew Little. I am also most grateful to Mr Charles Stadden for permission to use his research material on early uniforms and weapons; to Maj A J Hawley RM for his comments on this typescript and Capt D A Oakley RM for his revision of the galleys. A number of individuals kindly provided detailed accounts of events described in chapters 7 and 8. And while I hope those who read these sections of the book will accept my general thanks and excuse my not naming them individually, I am particularly indebted to Colonel R C Sidwell OBE for his detailed help with several actions described in chapter 7.

J D Ladd

Chapter 1

Ship Actions, Assaults and Sieges

The sullen clouds of a winter's day merged with the line of breakers ahead, beyond which the lookouts could just make out a Dutch sail. For Will Derby, a private in the Admiral's Regiment, the roll of drums calling the crew to action brought him scrambling down from the foremast shrouds and the cold monotony of peering uncertainly through the gloom. He went below to fetch a firelock. After the Corporal handed him one from the chest below decks, the musket was soon loaded, the powder rammed from one of his 'Apostle' charges followed by a leaden ball.

The Blue Squadron of which Will Derby's ship was one, had stayed in the Narrow Seas when the rest of the English fleet returned to St Helens Roads (Portsmouth). They had been at sea four days since 27 November 1664, allowing Will time to recover from his early seasickness and unsteadiness. He was back on the quarterdeck before the Corporal had ranged the musketeers along the larboard barrier (bulwark). Two Dutch ships were clearly visible, making for a channel they must have known between the breakers, but the Captain of Will's ship had stood close inshore and would cut them off though whether or not he would attempt to take them as prizes was in doubt. There was no state of war between the two nations, although since the peace treaty of 1654 there had been incidents: English ships boarded in the Spanish Main, Dutchmen driven from their forts on the west African coast, and many a Dutch captain had refused to acknowledge English ships as the treaty required. The two Dutchmen, here off the Texel coast,

probably did not fire a salute or dip their flags, but instead sailed boldly on.

A warning round might be answered by the Hollanders' firing into the English ships' rigging, but details of such actions have not come down to us. We do know that the English bought or captured several thousand Dutch ships which formed the core of their merchant fleet after 1660. In these actions[1] the Dutchmen with their relatively nimble shallow-drafted ships still favoured boarding enemy vessels, while the English, with heavier cannon, relied on pounding their enemy into submission. Men like Will Derby therefore (although he himself is fictitious) had been trained, albeit briefly, to carry out those seamen's jobs which required a number of men to work in unison, such as, for example, hauling a wrecked mizzen mast clear of the after deck when the Hollanders had shot it away.

Will Derby may be fictitious, but we do know that in the early winter of 1664 the first English Maritime Regiment was raised. Charles II – a scheming if inconsistent politician – saw advantages in sea soldiers. They were paid by Parliament and had joined for life whereas seamen only signed on for a voyage; consequently the Regiment would become, intentionally or by accident, a nursery for seamen. Parliament had no objection to this 'standing' (or regular) naval force, although always hostile to a standing army, which might repress the English.

The Duke of York and Albany's Maritime Regiment of Foot was raised on 28 October 1664 and within five weeks 250 of its men were at sea as part of the English forces being brought together for

*At the Court at Whitehall
the 28th of October 1664.

Present

The King's most Excellent Ma.tie*

His Royall Highness y.e Duke of York.
Lord Chancellor
Lord Treasurer
Duke of Albemarle
Duke of Ormond
Lord Chamberlain
Earle of Anglesey
Earle of Lauderdaill

Earle of Middleton
Lord B.pp of London
Lord Ashley
M.r Vice Chamberlain
M.r Secretary Morice
M.r Secretary Bennet
M.r Chancellor of y.e Dutchy
S.r Edward Nicholas

The Order in Council of 28 October 1664 which established the first British regiment of sea soldiers, the forerunners of the Royal Marines. With spelling modernised, the Order reads in part: 'Upon a report from . . . the commissioners for the affairs of His Majesty's Naval Royal and Admiralty . . . His Majesty was pleased to order . . . that twelve hundred land soldiers be forthwith raised . . . to be distributed in His Majesty's fleets . . . to be put in one Regiment . . . divided into six companies . . . The care of all which is recommended to the Duke of Albermarle . . .'

*Land Soldiers to be
raysed to serve in his
Ma.ts fleets at Sea
1200*

Upon a Report from the Lords the Com.tie for the Affayres of his Ma.tie Navy Royall & Admiralty of this Kingdome this day read at the Boare: His Ma.tie was pleased to Order and direct (amongst other things) That twelve hundred Land Soldiers be forthwith rayded, to be in readiness, to be distributed into his Ma.ts ffleets prepared for Imploym.t: The said twelve hundred Men are to be putt into One Regiment, Under One Colonell, One Lieutenant Colonell & One Serjeant Major And to be devided into Six Companies, Each Company to consist of Two hundred Soldiers; And to have One Captain, One Lieutenant, One Ensigne, One Drumer, ffower Serjeants, & ffower Corporalls, And all the Soldiers aforesaid to be armed with good firelocks: All w.ch Armes Drums & Colours are forthwith to be prepared and furnished out of his Ma.ties Stoares: The care of all which is recommended to the Duke of Albemarle his Grace Lord Generall of his Ma.ts fforces.

the coming war with Holland. Their six companies (see Appendix 2) and staff totalled 1,286 all ranks, the senior officers also being company commanders following the practice of that time.

The companies were armed with firelocks (fusils) – the musket of the two fusilier companies with Cromwell's artillery train – but did not carry pikes. This last was one of several differences between army soldiers and the Admiral's Regiment (as the Regiment was also known). Arming the Regiment had been

(not for the last time!) a slow process, since the mechanism of their firelocks were made by hand, the gunsmiths at the Tower of London working to provide 1,000 of these special muskets that winter. Some 250, however, had reached Southampton in November 1664, coming by cart from London. The following year the Regiment's distinctive yellow coats and uniform were first issued. Yellow was the Duke of York's favourite colour but more probably was chosen for its similarity to the tawny, yellow-brown coats of Cromwell's fusiliers. The familiar red coat would not be worn until the Regiment of 1686 adopted it (see Appendix 2).

The Admiral's Regiment was to be assembled at Southampton as quickly as possible, the officers being commissioned in the Regiment on 5 November 1664. The companies, whose captains were responsible for the men's pay, were to be paid out of funds provided by Parliament as soon as each company was ready for sea or for service in the dockyards; the Regiment was to be billeted in the inns and houses of the major English ports where they would not only provide garrisons but would also fit-out warships.

At least 250 of the first recruits into the Regiment had previously been soldiers and arrived at Southampton in the remnants of old uniforms. Some had served in the recently abolished Trained Bands of London, which had been militia raised by the City Corporation to defend London against Parliamentary forces if necessary. Others of the recruits, no doubt, had been in Cromwell's army, for the Regiment had both Catholics and Protestants among its officers and rank-and-file. Each man carried his few possessions tied up in a piece of cloth or a sack, many were 'on the road' having slept under hedgerows or in cheap lodgings. Their average age was about 19; they had joined for the bounty and the promise of prize money.

The versatility of these sea soldiers – they were not called Marines until 1672 – has left its mark on the Royal Marines commando of the 1980s. It was during the 17th century that the Marines' ability to both fight ashore as infantry and take their full part in manning warships was firmly established. Their discipline, of a high order, came to be favourably compared to seamen of those days and was enforced by hard if fair regulations. The early Quarter-Master Marshalls (sic), for example, had the power before 1689 to hang privates as the ultimate punishment.

The Regiment provided detachments for sea service, when the men wore seaman's rig, or largely so. The broad-brimmed hat and heavy coat were not the clothes to wear in a ship's rigging, and the shoes – fitting left or right foot equally well or badly – were too poor a fit for agile work, so the men went barefoot. They were recruited by their company commanders. For example, Sir Edward Charlton, at 49, raised 'his company of stout young men of Tynedale all armed' before he marched them to Newcastle. Sir Edward, a Royal favourite, apparently provided their muskets before the Company was officially formed and placed on the Regiment's muster roles.

This company was one of the six raised in 1666. Yet so many sea soldiers were transferring to naval service as foremast hands, that the captains had great difficulty keeping their companies up to strength. No money was paid by Parliament for recruiting replacements nor for the bounties that might induce them to join. Other losses through sickness and action had also to be replaced, and the death rate was high. In the *Assistance*, for example, 200 men were crowded on this 56-gun 4th-Rate, only 40m long, with waste material, human and vegetable, festering in her bilges, nor had plague rats' fleas far to jump in spreading disease.

In garrison duties the Company Commander was often appointed Governor of the fort with its guns manned by his men. This was certainly true of Colonel Lyttleton, who in 1666 was commanding Landguard fort across the river Orwell from Harwich, its three batteries on projecting ramparts, covering the approach to this harbour and dockyard. These defences would be tested the following year, after Dutch Marines came ashore. They had already attacked ships and harbours in the Thames estuary, where Sir John Griffith's company among others held them from the Gravesend anchorage by his 'new line of batteries' with some 80 guns. Expecting further landings on the east coast, the English had concentrated six companies of the Regiment at Harwich. They were not kept waiting long, for on 1 July 1667 a Dutch fleet of over 40 ships

Soldiers in the colourful uniforms of the early Maritime Regiments. *Left to right*: An officer of the Lord High Admiral's Regiment, 1664–85; A soldier of the Prince George of Denmark's Regiment after they adopted the red coat with yellow facings in 1686; A private of the Lord High Admirals Regiment. From illustrations by an unknown artist in Major L. Edye RMLI's *Historical Records of the Royal Marines* Vol. 1.

anchored off the port beyond the range of Landguard Fort, while English block-ships across the Orwell were prepared for scuttling.

At dawn next day the Dutch fleet weighed anchor, running north-east past Felixstowe before turning back towards Harwich. They had the advantage as in those days (before troops could be moved quickly over land) a seaborne force might be put ashore virtually unopposed in landings where the defenders could not be concentrated. This the Dutch did, coming 'within half a cannon shot . . . below Filstowe Cliffe (sic)', that is: 1.5km or so off the beach south of Felixstowe and still out of range of Landguard Fort. Here in the early afternoon they put ashore 3,000 men, while eight or more ships engaged the Fort and sent clouds of smoke on the northerly breeze to blot out the garrison's view of the landing.

Five hundred Dutchmen climbed to higher ground beyond the cliff, where they positioned two 3-pounders to cover the lanes and hedgerows leading to the woods above their beachhead. By four o'clock the local militia were advancing in close order against this defence, but the English cavalry could not deploy in the woods and Dutch pikemen stood off the militiamen.

Meanwhile several hundred Hollanders marched briskly along the coast track, cutlasses drawn, to come out of the smoke at Landguard Fort. They were met by the steady fire of two companies of the Admiral's Regiment, who held the attackers for half an hour, preventing them putting their 7-metre scaling ladders against the walls before they withdrew. For some time they recovered their breath in the cover of sand dunes near the Fort and were peppered by shot from three small English ships. About 5.30 the raiders made a second assault but were again repulsed, the garrison apparently making a sally, for the Dutch retired in haste, leaving ladders, grenades and 'a case of very handsome pistols' as they retreated in some disorder along the Salt Road up the coast. Nevertheless the Dutch beachhead was maintained until the early hours of next morning, as the flood tide did not float off their ships' boats until 2 am. They had lost over 150 killed but there had been only six casualties in the Fort, despite the bombardment and in-

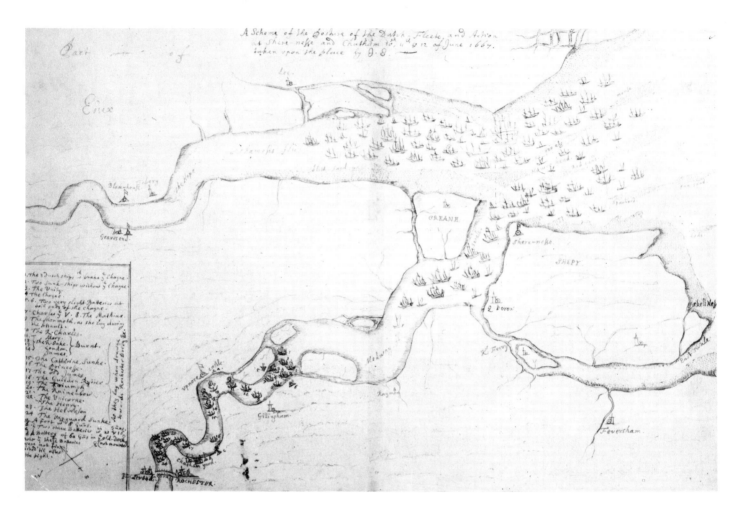

A scheme of the position of the Dutch fleet and action at Sheerness and Chatham on 10, 11 and 12 of June 1667 sketched by John Evelyn. The Dutch landed soldiers and Marines, captured Sheerness on 10 June and attacked Chatham burning several ships on 12 June. They attempted to sail from the Medway into the Thames but were blocked at Gravesend by the line of batteries commanded by Sir John Griffiths of the Admiral's Regiment. Sir John and his company had built these batteries earlier in the month and held the line with the help of reinforcements from London. From a sketch map by John Evelyn in the Bodleian Library, Oxford.

fantry attacks. (In the 1980s the successors to these Dutch soldiers and Marines serve with 3 Commando Brigade in Norway.)

This was the last time that Marines fought on English soil. They were to fight overseas throughout much of the next three centuries, but within the first few years of the Regiment's formation, they had established what would become traditional roles: fighting in ships' detachments when their country needed to strengthen her naval forces; and at other times being deployed to meet the strategic needs for additional army troops. Little is known of their individual roles in early sea battles, but detachments were in the fleet which overwhelmed the Dutch in June 1665 at the battle of Lowestoft, the Four Day Fight, the following year. Off Southwold in the battle of Solebay in 1672, when the *Royal James* was set alight by a fireship slipped from the lee of the Dutch flagship, Capt Thomas Bromley of

the Regiment was lost with the *Royal James*; but his Ensign, after swimming for an hour, was saved 'his head a little burnt and his mouth hurt'. Three other Marine captains were killed in this action.

John Churchill 'that was ensigne [sic] to ye King's Company', replaced one of the Marine captains killed at Solebay. Although he was only 22 when appointed to the Regiment, John Churchill was an officer of great promise and as Duke of Marlborough would fight brilliant campaigns in Europe. His company and several others from the Admiral's Regiment joined a battalion with army companies in France, and by 1674 some 550 Marines were serving there. The formation of units, especially for overseas service in the late 17th century, was frequently based on battalions of companies from different regiments. The Admiral's Regiment, for example, provided 200 men for a company joining an army battalion in

Virginia. These Marines were drawn from existing companies, but the Virginia Company was not at full strength when it sailed in October 1676. The men served there for some two years on what would now be called 'internal security duties' at the end of which 20 men joined the settlers.

On their return to England in 1679 the Virginia Company were trained as grenadiers. Grenadiers were special troops for storming defences and were usually of above average height and equipped with hand-thrown bombs lit from a slow-match. All Marines came to be regarded as grenadiers although not necessarily armed as such. A regular grenadier company did not serve in the Regiment until 1685, by which time the Regiment had changed its name to Prince George's Regiment or the Prince's Regiment. The loyalty of their senior officers to Parliament was in question, however, for their

Colonel, Sir James Lyttleton, was a one-time Royalist spy and a courtier friend of the Duke of York, who had been crowned James II in February 1685. James II fled the country in the Glorious Revolution of 1688 and the Regiment was therefore disbanded in 1689.

New regiments would be formed, however (see Appendix 2). Although for some years these early Marines had frequently been employed as army troops, the Admiralty became less ready to release them in the 1690s. For in that decade new designs of ships were able to stay at sea through the rough northern winters rather than spend October to March in their home ports. Long voyages blockading French and other coasts were to become a feature of British strategy in wartime, with the Maritime Regiments serving 'aboard their Majesties' ships as well in winter as in summer'. The practice of naval officers serving also as company

The *Royal James* under attack from three fire boats and the *Groot Hollandia* of 60 guns in the battle of Solebay, 28 May 1672, when the Dutch attacked an English fleet commanded by the Lord High Admiral. The *Royal James* of 100 guns had been commissioned the previous year and carried a crew of over 500 and a company of the Admiral's Regiment of about 70 all ranks. Painting by P. Monamy, National Maritime Museum, London.

The Four Days Fight was one of the longest and most hard fought sea battles. It took place off the Netherlands' coast between a Dutch fleet and English squadrons commanded by the Lord High Admiral and Prince Rupert. The 78 English ships carried 21,000 seamen and men of the Admiral Regiment; 5,000 of these crews were lost with 17 ships before the English broke off the engagement on 4 July (modern 14 July) 1666. Painting by P. C. van Soest, National Maritime Museum, London.

commanders in the Regiments (a practice begun in 1671) became so prevalent in this period, that regulations had to be made against it. But for the men there were few changes.

They continued to be billeted in houses and inns, for which their hosts received 4d (2p) a man per day. Some billeting 'rackets' must have developed for after 1685 sergeants were prohibited from keeping inns or victualling houses. And discipline was further improved in 1690, when officers for the first time were ordered to find quarters near the men's billets. The Marines marched 20km a day, with a rest day every third or fourth, and were 'rehearsed at the great guns', as although these Marines were not gunners they hauled on the gun ropes or carried shot at sea when necessary. They became good musket shots, despite the limited quantities of powder for practice (balls could be re-cast) as 17th century Parliaments were as bound by financial stringencies as their successors. This skill was put to good use at sea, since enemy guns could be as readily disabled by picking off the crew as by a cannon shot dismounting the gun.

Ashore their musketry was also used to good effect. At the siege of Cork in September 1690, four Marine sharpshooters killed the Irish colonel and many of his men in a key fort of the defences. Their duties ashore also involved internal security, for example supporting the rule of law in Jamaica in 1692. Three years later they were in action at Cape Passero (Sicily) where Royal Marine commandos would land in 1943. But some examples of their smaller operations between 1664 and 1755 are summarised in the notes.[1]

The first major operation of the 18th century in which numbers of Marines (now six regiments raised in 1702) were in action was the seizing of Gibraltar. The English had taken up the cause of Archduke Charles of Austria in his claim to the Spanish throne, while France supported the claim of King Philip V. To support the Archduke, Sir George Rooke, who had

held a commission in the Marines, was sent with Dutch and English ships to besiege Cadiz. Local forces, however, did not rise to the Archduke's help, and the Allies withdrew. It was now early in October 1702 and a Spanish treasure convoy had reached Vigo (north Spain) some weeks earlier. Sir George therefore tacked north some 1,000km against headwinds, to reach their anchorage in five days.

The ships were protected by a boom of rafts, spars chained together in great bundles 3m in diameter. Thirteen French warships, batteries of shore guns and some 10,000 Spanish troops also protected the treasure ships. But on 11 October, in foggy weather, the English and Dutch put ashore 2,000 troops including 1,000 Marines who marched 10km across rough hills to seize the 40-gun fort of Redonella, enabling English ships to crash the boom and force the enemy ships to scuttle or run aground. A great deal of silver bullion was taken in a victory which foreshadowed the seizing of Gibraltar nearly two years later. This had been in the fleet's original orders for 1702 but was cancelled 'as the season of the year is so advanced'.

Gibraltar with its 300m Rock dominating the straits over 15km wide, was prized as 'the greatest thoroughfare of trade'. Cromwell had seen its value in 1656, Charles II had considered its capture and Queen Anne's Ministers knew its value. Yet the Spanish had only a small garrison of 150 regulars and 350 militia stationed there, believing that their 100 cannon could be expected to hold the fortified town.

Sir George Rooke's second expedition left England on 5 January 1704 with over 5,000 English and Dutch troops, to land the Archduke, after duly rehearsed ceremony, at Lisbon, where he was welcomed by the King of Portugal. The fleet then sailed, at the Archduke's request, to pass through the straits of Gibraltar and land 2,000 men at Barcelona in north-east Spain, some five days' march from the French border. But the English were only ashore a day, while the Dutch landed to bombard the town, before the threat of a superior force caused them to withdraw on 19 May.

They sailed south, landing 900 marines four miles from Malaga to secure a watering point, since the fleet needed fresh water and fuel for the galley fires every four or five weeks. The troops were ashore here from 7–9 July, the seaman working-parties being unarmed and kept to their task under threat of the Marine sentries firing on anyone leaving the watering points. This did not stop men gathering onions nor four Frenchmen, understandably, deserting from the 2nd Marines. (Although Marine Regiments were known by their Colonel's name at this time [see Appendix 2] their numbers are more easily identified and have therefore been used here.) The service of foreigners in English regiments was not new, and until 1810 there would be many, including former prisoners of war, on the muster rolls of Marine Regiments.

Senior naval officers joined Marine officers ashore, Admiral Dilkes doing a little fishing and Admiral Byng handsomely entertaining several officers in a captured mill house. There were a few skirmishes with Spanish cavalry but only two seamen were killed, and as they were 'in an onion garden' they had probably disobeyed orders. Before the shore parties rejoined their ships, they set fire to a number of mills including one holding 10,000 bushels (c400 tonnes) of corn, and burnt down several houses. The Spaniards appeared as Marine covering parties held the final beachhead under cover of bombardment from several frigates.

The Allied fleet then passed westward through the Straits and on 16 July rendezvoused with Admiral Sir Cloudesley Shovel's squadron, which joined them at the anchorage in Lagos Bay (southern Portugal). Sir George 'a cautious and difficult man' baulked at attacking Cadiz, and Sir Cloudesley sailed back east through the Straits. The main fleet followed the next day, making some five knots to the anchorage 50km south east of Gibraltar on the Moroccan coast. The weather was hot with little wind when the officers of Col Fox's Regiment, 3rd Marines, were called to the *Boyne* for orders, as no doubt were Col Luttrel's officers of the 2nd Marines. Since February the land forces with the fleet had been commanded by Prince Hesse of Darmstadt, an ancestor of Lord Mountbatten, and the Prince had decided to attack Gibraltar, with which Sir George agreed.

Each Marine was to land with 18 charges – not much perhaps but a firelock could only be fired at some three rounds every two minutes. Company COs each had a reserve of cartridges and shot carried by a Marine in one of the large cannon cartridge-cases used aboard ship, the leather sling over his shoulder. The men in the grenadier companies, one with each Regiment, carried two grenades.

During the afternoon of Sunday 21 July the vanguard of the 40 English ships anchored in 20m of water before the town less than 2km from the shore. The Prince led the English and Dutch Marines ashore on the isthmus some hours later 700m north of the ramparts. The close support fire of small ships drove off a few Spanish cavalry and by nightfall the Marines were established in three mills. That night a party of seamen and Marines from the ships' detachments (Fleet Marines) rowed in and set fire to a ship moored at the north (Old) mole that had been able to fire diagonally, in enfilade, across the Marines' front. While it was dark the vanguard of the English and Dutch ships for a second time also moved closer to the shore, small boats laying anchors ahead of the craft which were then hauled up to them, until in some cases there was only 30cm of water under the larger vessels. As they each completed this manoeuvre, the ships fired shot, mortar bombs and some 'carcasses' into the town. The last named were iron-bound canvas cylinders covered in pitch and filled with combustibles, i.e. 18th-century incendiary bombs.

A view of the Rock of Gibraltar from the French and Spanish lines in 1704. Marines had captured the Rock in July 1704 and held it under an intensive siege which was not lifted until April 1705. Painting by N. Ozanne, RM Museum, Eastney.

At dawn next day, Monday, the ships began a heavy bombardment, firing 1,500 rounds in a few hours, and by 10 am fires were burning in the town. Meanwhile from the force of 1,900 British and 400 Dutch Marines, companies advanced despite enemy fire, cutting off the Spanish garrison from reinforcements. The Governor had refused to surrender, for he was expecting a French and Spanish relief force, and almost all the women and children were safely on the mainland.

About midday, when the Spanish gunners had been driven from the south mole batteries, seamen rowed ashore to seize it. On this mole was an arsenal supplying its 22 cannon and not long after the seamen landed the powder in this store exploded. Possibly a seaman's slow match had been dropped among the loose powder, or the Spanish fired a mine they had ready on the mole, but whatever the cause, the blast

the north mole's battery, which they captured under covering fire from the ships. The Governor did not formally agree to surrender until that evening, but there was little firing during the day's truce; and the few women found in the chapel were escorted out of the town so that they would not be molested. The garrison were allowed to march out with the honours of war – a chivalry that among professional armies could prevent the unnecessary loss of life in prolonged sieges. The Prince had Archduke Charles' flag raised, but Admiral Rooke replaced it with the English flag, taking possession of the Rock of Gibraltar in the name of Queen Anne. In the aftermath, several men were caught together stealing goods and one Englishman hung as an example, the men having thrown dice for the punishment: 'a Dutchman hove ten, and an Englishman nine'. Other would-be looters were rounded up by patrols of officers and sergeants, who sent them back to the ships.

Admiral Rooke sailed a few days later to water on the Moroccan coast, leaving the Prince of Hesse in command of the Marines' garrison. They would later be reinforced by Guardsmen and other troops, but for the next 12 months Marines provided the main defence of the Rock.

The Admiral, having sent back for 1,000 Marines from the garrison, relieved the immediate threat of a French attack from the sea, when he found their fleet in Malaga Bay. In a day-long battle, the fleets bombarded each other from 10 am until 7 pm as they sailed southward on parallel courses during 12 August. No ship was lost but over 2,000 men were killed in each fleet. The English had been running out of ammunition, but on the Monday, 13 August, the French sailed for Toulon.

Admiral Rooke returned to Gibraltar on 19 August where Marines helped to repair his ships. They had already, in less than four weeks, made good Gibraltar's defences, mounting 42 guns on the south

killed 150 seamen and some Spaniards. Many of the boats 'were staved in pieces' and others began rowing for the ships. But no Spaniards appeared and two naval captains led their men ashore. In a short time they had taken the chapel 'with its rich plunder which the captains shared . . . and took away that which the seamen had got'.

The Marines meanwhile had advanced from the siege trenches to within 80m of

mole and installing new batteries at the town gate, the Land Port, at the north-west corner of the town's walls. These walls were repaired, and the Round Tower 300m north of them was refortified to cover the only track leading to the Land Port. Under the direction of Capt Bennett of the army's engineers, flanking trenches were built to run south-eastward to the Rock's cliff face, and another trench linked the Land Port to the Tower. This communication was defensively mined in October with four chambers charged with powder barrels, the powder trail running 150m to the Covered Way, a defence work behind the protective slope of an embankment built by the Spanish against bombardment. Rooke had sailed for England on 25 August but it was not until 9 October that a Spanish army of 3,000 began digging major siege works.

These works were 700m from the Round Tower but could not span the isthmus for the Marines had flooded its low-lying east side by breaking the sea wall. The Spanish guns, nevertheless, engaged the Marines' batteries which their 100 seamen gunners and armourers helped to keep in action. As Gibraltar's walls became breached, a second line behind the flanking trench was built with revetments of earth piled against wooden frames on the north-west slopes of the Rock. But the Spanish guns had reduced the Round Tower to a mound of rubble, and by now the 9,000 Spaniards on the isthmus were further reinforced by 4,500 Frenchmen and 1,200 Walloons, as German mercenaries were known. They had brought 200 small boats from Cadiz, planning to attack the defences at the same time as 3,000 men were landed on the south mole on the night of 25 October, but that afternoon Admiral Leake arrived on his second relief attempt, his first attempt having been driven off by French ships. This time he landed 200 barrels of powder, seven months' rations and 400 Marines, and as his ships came into the bay, they sank or drove ashore several French ships. Any seaborne attack on the south mole

would, therefore, be unprotected and so the Spanish called off their assault.

The Spaniards, however, did make one attempt to infiltrate men behind the English batteries, a goatherd guiding 500 men up the east facing cliffs of the Rock, where there was no continuous line of defences. The leading party scaled this cliff with ropes at night, and the remainder followed up rope ladders to lay up in caves until first light. Just before dawn they rushed the signal station on the crest of the Rock, killing the sentries. Lt-Col Bor, second-in-command of the 3rd Marines, led eight Marine companies to dislodge them. The action was short, if sharp, for the Spaniards had only three rounds apiece, being forced to hurl rocks in their defence before surrendering after 200 were killed. Bor would later succeed Col Fox, when the latter was killed on 11 November with the Governor of the Rock during one of the many bombardments that winter. Col Bor, 39 years old at the time, was greatly respected as a fair man who 'had great compassion on a soldier' or Marine. Something of a character, he was killed in 1723 by his own bloodhound when he lost a wager that the dog could recognise him in any disguise.

Secondary earthworks had been built around breaches in the walls with rubble piled each night from one large breach to make a defended mound and from this and other revetments, the defenders could engage men coming through a breach. The Spaniards also improved their trenches, and despite illumination from barrels of blazing tar rolled each night towards their lines, managed to get these to within 30m of the Tower and revetments around its base. They used 'chandeliers' (frameworks holding bundles of stout sticks) to protect parties working at night, but were greatly hampered by rain which would flood the low ground by January. This wet weather also caused their artillery many misfires, and on the English side guns had to be manhandled 'in gears' (sledge-like cradles) across marshy ground, before laying spars over rock in order to haul the guns to the batteries, using ropes and tackles.

Further English reinforcements arrived in December including Guardsmen and some Portuguese troops, 2,000 in all. But the Marine Regiments were down to 1,000 men as many were sick, others casualties and some had been withdrawn to strengthen ships' crews. Conditions in the town had become difficult but some food reached the garrison from Spain, as smugglers brought it by small boats, for sale on the Rock. While afloat the marine companies had each been allowed to bring three wives. These women helped the surgeon when a ship was in action, and at other times laundered clothes for the company, doing some cooking and what little was done to keep their quarters clean, no doubt. Some of these women were probably also landed to take care of the sick at Gibraltar.

As the defence works were not a continuous line but a series of sentry posts to the east, messengers could smuggle intelligence when they landed in small boats. In this way, probably, a Spanish colonel while a prisoner was 'corresponding with the enemy', and when discovered was shot. Two other spies were English civilians 'put out of town . . . with halters round their necks'. Messages for a friar were intercepted by 'out sentries' and two Majors were executed for betraying the garrison. How far it was possible to get through the lines is not clear, but there were raids mounted by Marines; and after the December reinforcement the Prince of Hesse led two major night raids. On the first, 300 men destroyed over 60m of Spanish breastworks, and the second was equally successful with only a few losses on each occasion.

These raids and the cost of the bombardment led the Spanish to mount a major assault late in January 1705 in order to finish the siege. They first made a fighting reconnaissance with 50 grenadiers, each carrying a hook in one hand to climb the rubble against a breach near the Round Tower, where an old wall ran towards the beach. This breach was covered by outposts manned each night by 90 men of a reinforced captain's company with three subalterns. But at dawn each day 60 of these men and the captain were withdrawn into defences around the Round Tower, where Col Bor had a garrison of 180.

Before dawn, one day late in January, 500 French and Walloon grenadiers infiltrated past the Tower 'to the hollows and clits' (folds) on the lower slopes of the Rock. When they saw the captain withdraw to the Tower, the grenadiers attacked the outposts, while 300 of them attacked the Tower. They climbed the old wall and fired down into the trenches by the Tower, cutting off Col Bor from the town. He led his men over the revetments around the Tower and back to the Covered Way. Capt Fisher (4th Marines) turned back to cover this withdrawal 'leading 17 men against 500', but was captured along with those of his men who were not killed. However the alarm had been raised throughout the garrison and Col Moncall of Lord Barrymore's Regiment of the line led 400 men down the communication trench to the Tower. Their advance was covered by English grenadiers of the Guards who had climbed up the Rock from the Covered Way to get musket fire onto the enemy on the old wall. Within an hour the Tower was recaptured but confused fighting continued for a while, and Capt Fisher having been released by the counter-attack was again taken prisoner.

Had the 1,000 Spanish infantry intended to support the grenadiers followed up the initial attack, they might have broken into the defences. As it was, this and a later attack in February by 18 companies of French and Spanish troops failed to recapture the town. At sea Admiral Leake's ships surprised a squadron of French ships-of-the-line capturing three, and on 10 March landed sufficient reinforcements and supplies to secure the Rock. By this date the Spanish were short of ammunition, ill-clothed, ill-paid and

On the disbandment of the 4th Marines in 1713 a number joined the navy as foremast hands. They saw action in the battle of Cape Passero (Sicily) on 11 August 1718 when Admiral Byng's squadron chased 20 Spanish ships and captured 11 of them. In World War II RM Commandos made the initial assault on this cape in 1943. Painting by R. Paton; National Maritime Museum, London, Greenwich Hospital Collection.

without fodder for their horses, so the siege was raised on 18 April. Despite the small Spanish force left to guard the isthmus, fresh supplies reached the Rock from Spain.

In July the seasoned companies of Marines (now in four battalions) joined the fleet, and two army regiments were landed. The fleet with its convoy of transports carrying 10,000 men, sailed for Barcelona, invested the city and after some weeks captured it. The Prince of Hesse, who had been an inspiration to his men in Gibraltar, was killed. Col Bor was also wounded fighting a duel with Col Rodney (2nd Marines) before their assembled regiments after the initial landing. Rodney was killed, but the incident did not affect Bor's career as he must have been gravely provoked.

During the conclusion of this War of the Spanish Succession and later when fresh regiments were raised in 1739 (see Appendix 2), Marines not only fought as detachments on ships, but were often used to seize and later garrison naval bases. Six Regiments were sent to Jamaica in 1740, where they were joined by two

Colonial Marine Regiments[2] commanded by Col William Gooch, a 58-year-old veteran of Marlborough's great victory at Blenheim. They sailed with the Marine Regiments for Cartegena (Columbia) where the Colonial Marines were at first employed as pioneers, but many took up arms when the going got tough.

Dilatory leadership, yellow fever and strong Spanish defences, took a heavy toll of the expedition's troops, although the Colonial Marines had been expected to withstand the climate better than the British. But over 1,400 of the Americans were casualties by the October, after 500 reinforcements had been absorbed into the companies. Only one in ten of the British marines survived.

The British Marine Regiments of 1739 were disbanded in 1748, after the drafting of men to ships' detachments had led to a confusion of mixed regiments. Nevertheless the value of Marines had been established as a force which could be deployed both by sea and land according to their country's needs, and a permanent Corps was therefore raised in 1755 consisting of 50 independent companies.

Chapter 2

Amphibious Strategy and Infantry Actions: Belle Isle and America

The Corps of Marines formed in 1755 was made up of 50 independent companies each of 100 privates – they were stationed at the principal naval dockyard ports: 20 companies at Portsmouth, 18 at Plymouth and 12 at Chatham forming the three Grand Divisions. It was at these ports that ships of the fleet were fitted out, the companies providing detachments and from time to time battalions to supplement battalions of 'Fleet' Marines drawn from the detachments in ships. When the Seven Years War broke out in 1756, the number of companies was doubled and some men were signed on 'for the duration' or a minimum of three years.

They were to spend long periods away from their home ports, in the ships blockading the European ports, and although they received some training in the companies many went to sea ill-prepared. The two battalions formed in 1760–61, however, appear to have had some military training in army drills adapted for sea service 'with barricade fire to repel boarders', before they joined an army force of 6,500 which sailed under secret orders to attack Belle Isle off Quiberon Bay on the Brittany coast. This would provide an advanced base for the blockading ships and be a threat to the French coast, forcing the French to withdraw troops from Germany where they were attacking Britain's allies. However the few landing points on the islands rocky shores were strongly defended.

After a rough passage the assault force was off the island on 6 April 1761 and two days later bombarded the principal town of Palais dominated by its great citadel. That morning ships slipped away from the main fleet, taking 500 Marines north along the coast where they transferred to 'flats' (the landing barges of those days) but did not land. Other flats put ashore a force of soldiers on the south coast. They were met by heavy French fire and repulsed with 425 casualties. The weather deteriorated and many of the flats were damaged since they were stowed on the open decks of the transports. Replacements were received with reinforcements from England and a second landing planned for 22 April. This would again be on the south coast, near the point below Fort d'Arsic where the first landings were repulsed. This time, however, a secondary landing would be made nearby at Luc Maria Bay, while feints would be made elsewhere to discourage the French from concentrating their defence force near Luc Maria.

Wednesday 22 April dawned a misty morning, as the main fleet came inshore to bombard Fort d'Arsic before the troops transferred into flats early in the afternoon. Each Marine carried his Brown Bess musket, slung across his shoulder 'to prevent it being lost in getting aboard'. It weighed 14lb (6.3kg) against the modern Self Loading Rifle's 4.3kg, but at Belle Isle a Marine carried about two-thirds of the 27kg carried by a Marine in action in the 1980s. The Marine companies (one in every two or three flats or ships' boats) wore their equipment strapped on for action, not the parade ground. Bayonets were buckled on the right shoulder, cartouche boxes with 18 charges a box were behind the left shoulder where the powder might keep dry.

As the flats were rowed northward

Commodore Keppel's ships put ashore English troops on 8 April 1761 in the initial unsuccessful landings near Fort d'Arsic, Belle Isle. Engraving after D. Serres.

along the coast, the French forces concentrated behind the beach below the fort. There they held the main assault force, while the Marines and grenadiers rowed further along the coast to land at the foot of a cliff near St Foy, on the north headland of Luc Maria Bay. The tensions of impending action were eased by activity in the boats: 'off lock covers' kept the men busy unwrapping the leather covers which had kept sea spray from the mechanisms of the muskets. Once ashore they were ordered to fix bayonets, but no

man would fire until ordered to do so. They were formed into files ready to clamber up the cliff, under the covering bombardment of HMS *Lynn* and *Hampton Court* whose cannons had been chocked up to get an elevation that reached the cliff-top defences.

An army company of Beauclerk's Regiment (19th) scaled the cliff, closely followed by Capt James Murray's company of Marines. To their left another company commander (possibly Capt A. Tooker Collins, who was the first Marine

ashore) ordered his men to take cover near the beach, and found a route up the cliff. Then, crawling forward on hands and knees, he located the French defences, before signalling his men to join him. Their Brown Bess muskets once again slung across their backs, they began the climb. Handholds on bushes, footing on tufts of grass, some slipped back at first and slithered down the cliff. Others found a way up the steep slope, all the time watching that their muskets did not bump against the cliff face, for mud on the flint

or pan would make these useless. A bayonet stayed firmly in place if you had 'doctored' the socket but one or two probably clattered down among those below, causing an oath or two. The French heard them, no doubt, but could not or did not fire over the cliff top. Then the marines were over the crest and beginning to form a line.

The first few companies had barely time to form this skirmish line at the cliff top before the French opened a steady fire on the Marines and other grenadiers, who

Major General Arthur Tooker Collins, first commissioned in the 3rd Marines in 1742, commanded a Marine battalion in the capture of Belle Isle. He later held a number of appointments in a distinguished career and died while Commandant at Plymouth, aged 80. Painting by an unknown artist on loan to CGRM from the general's family.

fired back. They reloaded squatting on their haunches behind what cover they could get, as they rammed home a fresh charge and musket ball, getting off four rounds every three minutes in the methodical drill at which veterans could fire even faster.

The fire 'became pretty brisk on both sides' before 300 Frenchmen of the Regiment de Bigorre charged from their breastworks along the line of a wall. The British formed up by squads (called 'platoons') to meet them. The leading squad of 14 men fired, turned into file and moved leftward up the higher ground on Loc Maria headland. Reloading in their new positions, they covered the movement of succeeding platoons.

General Lambert, who commanded this landing force, came ashore with the remainder of the assault troops, including Lt-Col Mackenzie's other Marine companies. They were able to climb cliffs to the left of the first landing, protected by fire from the advanced guard, although it was retreating further left. With these reinforcements the British charged the French, driving them back to the wall. Capt Paterson who had led the first army grenadiers up the cliff and Capt Murray of the Marines were both wounded. But the General and Col Mackenzie commanding the Marines now forced home a second charge, forcing the Regiment de Bigorre to fall back from the wall and join the men from Luc Maria. In this action Mackenzie was badly wounded and command of the Marine battalion passed to Maj Tooker Collins, promoted in the field.

Off the beach Commodore Keppel in his barge controlled the landing boats, which were now using beaches along the north side of the headland, because the main landing force under General Crauford, after being repulsed south of the bay, had been shipped to the north cliff beaches. Such flexibility in changing the point of the main assault, suggests that the General and Commodore worked closely together. By 5 pm, two hours into the assault, all the force was ashore. What little information

is available about the methods of co-ordinating the ships' bombardment, the movement of the flotillas and the change of plan, suggest that simple flag signals were used as well as flares.

That night the French defensive force lit a great beacon fire to signal the outlying garrisons of three regular battalions and one of militia to assemble in Palais. The British, 5km inland by nightfall, made camp on a hill among the islands' farms. Losses during the day had been slight, the men of the cliff assault losing 30 rank-and-

file killed or wounded and several officers wounded. French losses were probably the greater, some having been hit in the ships' bombardment.

Next day the British resumed their advance in several columns, and by evening were bivouacked only 2km from the Citadel, despite French attempts to delay them. Roads had been broken up, bridges destroyed and all the magazines of the coast batteries along the northern coast had been blown up. The next morning, Friday 24 April, the greater part of the

Fleet Marines were landed, initially to form a second Marine battalion. They came ashore through rough seas which prevented cannons being landed for several days; nor were axes, crowbars and shovels landed in quantity until the following Monday. Villages were then fortified and although some houses had been burnt down in the French retreat, local peasants were not unfriendly when given the prices they demanded for fresh produce.

The commander of the French garrison,

Reinforcements landed near Fort d'Arsic, Belle Isle on 8 April 1761 were unable to establish a beachhead and these army regiments were withdrawn. Engraving after D. Serres.

Marines capture the French redoubts guarding the approaches to the Palais Citadel in a dawn attack on 13 May 1761. Painting by Colonel C. Field, RM Museum, Eastney.

Chevalier de St Croix, was resolute in setting up defences and would prove 'the pink of Chivalry' as the siege developed. His soldiers had built six redoubts with earthworks over 5m thick in front of timbered frames – each about 300m apart. They formed a ring around the Citadel, 450 and 1,000m from it, with each redoubt covering natural approaches and tracks leading to the town.

During the first few days of May, a week after the British reached Palais, batteries were set up with trenches to protect them. General Crauford, the Army commander, was inspecting an outpost in front of these trenches, when on the night of 3 May 400 Frenchmen made a sally from the town, capturing the General and his two aides. The attackers were battling for the trench protecting the main battery of mortars and in hand-to-hand fighting the outcome was in the balance until Capt David Hepburn of the Marines led his

company in a bayonet charge which forced the French to retire.

Thirty Marines volunteered to take out the redoubt opposite the British right flank but were told to bide their time. They did not have to wait long, for at dawn on 13 May the British concentrated the fire from every cannon that would bear against this strong point. During darkness 30 4- to 6-inch brass mortars (Cohorns) and four guns had been moved into houses to the flank and rear of the redoubt, only 200m from it. They opened fire when the main bombardment stopped, just as Capt Walter Carruthers with Capt Smith (Loudon's Rgt, 30th) led a storming party of 200 Marines and soldiers out of the main British trench.

They advanced steadily across 400m of fields, crossed a road and with bayonets fixed prepared to charge the redoubt. Sixteen other Marines meanwhile man-handled their two field guns from the cover of the houses to the rear of the redoubt – a sweat of muscle and tension for they were exposed to fire from a second redoubt 220m from the first, but after the French fired two volleys they gave way.

The storming party saw the French retreat to the second and a third redoubt away to the left. Carruthers led his men towards the second, passing the Marine field guns, whose crews had two killed and seven wounded. This second redoubt was taken without difficulty, but the Marines were forced to withdraw at the third. Reserves of powder and shot were brought forward and the advance renewed; one volley followed up with a bayonet charge sent the French scurrying out of this third redoubt. British casualties had been less than 50 of which nine had been from the Marine field gun crews. The French lost considerably more including at least 800 from the Regiment du Nixe, many of whom were taken prisoner.

After two weeks of close bombardment a breach was at last opened in the walls large enough 'for the passage of a coach and four'. French sallies were unable to delay the inevitable assault, although on one occasion when Capt John Wright's company of Marines were nearly overwhelmed, his men with fierce determination, using bayonets and muskets, drove the French back. There were over 1,000 casualties in the citadel before negotiations for a truce began on the morning of 7 June and by 6 pm next evening the Articles of Capitulation were signed.

For their many acts of courage during the assault and siege, the Marines were awarded 'the distinction of wearing the laurel wreath on their colours and appointments'. The island was held as an advanced base for the British fleet until the peace of 1763; of more immediate importance to the war was that the French were compelled to reinforce their army at Quiberon Bay at the expense of their armies in Germany. For the Marines there would be many actions before the Seven Years War was over[1] including com-mando-type amphibious operations, and it is this element of the Corps' activities that we shall follow, with some occasional glimpses of the sea service that provided the foundation of the Marines' versatility. For they were to serve *per mare, per terram* (by sea, by land) as the Corps' motto describes.

After the Peace of Paris (February 1763) four out of every five Marines were demobilised (see Chapter 4, Note 4). This enabled the Admiralty to house the remainder in better quarters, the Marines taking over barracks in the dockyards for which they again provided guards. Another improvement was the appointment of Squad officers, who took over the administration of companies and the supervision of training – tasks formerly carried out by whoever was available from the sea-duty roster. Squad officers (chosen from officers on half pay in 1764) 'not only (needed) a thorough knowledge of accounts . . . but a minute exactness therein, as well as some experience of business'. They were replaced by Squad Sergeants in 1785 when the supply of 'necessaries for the whole Corps' was given by the Admiralty to one contractor. This supervision ensured that by the early 1770s field exercises were a regular part of training, but there was no major action in this decade until battalions were ordered to America.

The first indication the Corps received of the coming American fight for independence was in an Admiralty letter to the Divisions dated 3 October 1774. This asked for details of camp equipment available 'in a proper condition for use'. It was followed a few weeks later by orders for Major John Pitcairn to embark 460 Marines, mostly volunteers from Chatham, for Boston, Massachusetts.

Boston was the main British garrison in New England, and here the sometimes impulsive General Gage had his headquarters. He had served many years in the American Colonies, and understood the political situation in Boston better than the British government. The port's wooden houses were built on a headland joined to the mainland by a narrow isthmus, the Boston Neck, leading from Roxbury. Northward on a second headland lay Charlestown (population 2,700), across the 500m of harbour entrance, with Breed's Hill behind it adjoining Bunker Hill to the north-west. Immediately to the south of Boston was a third headland with three hills, the Dorchester Heights. In places there was only 500m of channel separating the shores of these headlands, which in winter were often joined by sea ice. Had this ice held in the cold weather of 1774–75, the Americans had planned to cross these waters and attack the British garrison, but the ice did not become strong enough.

When Major Pitcairn's Marines arrived the nearby heights of Bunker Hill and Dorchester had not been fortified by the British, perhaps because they did not wish to incite the Bostonians, but defence works had been built across the neck of the isthmus in front of Roxbury. (The original inlets and creeks around the old town were filled in many years later by demolishing hills surrounding it and land west of Boston Common reclaimed from the estuary.)

Although the Marines' ships arrived on 4 December they were not put ashore until the end of the month. Perhaps because they would be more comfortable aboard ship than in camp during the cold weather, for watchcoats and leggings were not available, essential clothing in temperatures of −30°C. It has been inferred that because there was a profit to be made by the Admiral from victualling the Marines aboard his ships, they were not landed. Certainly Major Pitcairn fretted to have them ashore. He was a portly Scotsman, aged 53, and had had army service before his commission in the Marines of 1756. One of his sons served in the Corps, the other was the midshipman who first sighted Pitcairn Island, named after his father in 1767. The close relationships of this old family from Fife gave the Major – a devout man – his sense of personal responsibility. One of several traits which endeared him to his men.

By spending Christmas aboard, the Marines had missed opportunities to celebrate ashore where rum was so cheap 'it debauched both Navy and Army'. On landing they were first deployed with the 43rd Regiment guarding the 'passage between Barton Point and Charlestown ferry', but by January they were attached to Brigadier-General Lord Percy's 1st Brigade, having received their watchcoats. The Major was appointed Military Commandant of Boston, and by his level headed attempts to cool the growing tensions of the coming spring 'endeared himself to the people' who sought him out in disputes because of his fairness and consideration.

In this capacity he accompanied several forays to capture rebel arms, the first (by sea in February 1775) failed in the intention to bring back cannons from Salem (32km north of Boston), but no blood was spilt as the Major extracted his 100 army troops from confrontation with rebels. On 18 April he accompanied the 800 strongbattalion of army grenadier and light companies with some Marines (although not by the original orders) which set out by river to seize arms in Concord, 20 miles (32km) by road from Boston.

The Rebels, expecting this raid, had a signal lantern burning in the North Church spire by 11 pm to warn their forces. The signal lamp – one for by water, two by land – was not the only warning, Paul Revere leaving Charlestown as the moon was rising at about 11 pm, rode to Lexington. He was a talented silversmith and made many valuable contributions to the American cause although these are less well known than his night ride towards Concord. The British companies had crossed the estuary of the Charles river to land at the isolated Phipps Farm by midnight and the light companies reached Lexington at sunrise (4.30 am).

The Major, hearing they were faced by some 500 armed men, rode quickly forward joining the advanced guard to find that a musket had been fired at them, but had 'flashed in the pan' as a misfire. There was nervousness on both sides as 'near 200 rebels . . . drawn up on the green . . . began to file off towards . . . stone walls on our right' as the Major rode within 100 metres of them. The British companies ran after them the Major calling to his men not to fire but to surround the rebels who numbered probably 70 Minutemen, the rest being spectators. Four or five shots came from behind the wall wounding a soldier and the Major's horse, which later threw him and he lost his pistols. Other shots came from the Meeting House to the Major's left, then (despite his orders and their officers' commands) 'the Light Infantry began a scattered fire'. These were the opening shots of the American War of Independence, which killed eight Americans, one Lexington man dying in the arms of his wife at the door of his cottage.

The British force pushed on six miles (10km) to Concord, destroyed three cannons, and dumped powder, flour and shot into the river, while the light companies were in action holding the Rebels from crossing two bridges west of the town. Their work done, the British fell back on Lexington and were attacked on all sides, before 1,400 reinforcements from the 1st Brigade, including Marines, reached Lexington about 2.30. The flank companies falling back to join them were exhausted and running out of ammunition – they had set out with 36 rounds apiece.

The relief force's two 6-pounders opened fire but it was 45 minutes before an organised column could begin the 24km march back to Boston. Lord Percy chose an unexpected route, heading for Bunker Hill but nevertheless Provincials 'concealed in houses and (others) advancing to within ten yards to fire' harassed the retreating British, who lost 65 killed, 178 wounded including two lieutenant-colonels, and 28 missing. Between 8 and 9 o'clock in the evening, the last stages of their retreat across the ferry from Charlestown to the Boston Camp was covered by

Somerset's guns and fleet marines, all of who had been landed. By this time the original force of light and grenadier companies had been on the move for most of the last 20 hours and in close contact with the enemy for 12 of them. The Americans' failure to cut them off stemmed more from a lack of military leadership than a reluctance to do battle, and would lull the British command into a false sense of superiority over the local militia.

The Americans had lost 49 killed and 366 wounded, but were greatly encouraged by this success. While the British in Boston, who now had a number of raw recruits and untrained junior officers in their ranks, were showing signs of indiscipline with a 'shameful neglect of guards, of centrys [sic] . . . and alertness at their posts'. Women with the Regiments also caused trouble although quarters had been found for them, some breaking into houses closed because of smallpox 'by which there is a danger of spreading (it) through the town'. British troops would not be inoculated against this disease until the following winter.

Rumour was rife and whether or not some wounded had been scalped in the retreat from Lexington, there were reports that they had been. This may not be as outrageous as it may seem to modern readers, as in the 1750s, for example, $130 was paid in Pennsylvania in bounty for every Indian scalp. Tales of the retreat no doubt reached the Marines of further companies landed in Boston on 15 May, the first contingent of 730 all ranks who had embarked in England on 25 March. The Plymouth detachment had paraded on the Barbican at 5.30 am that day, the men from Chatham had been almost entirely drawn from ships in the port, indeed about one-third of the force were Fleet Marines. They had brought with them 80 wives, some to join the companies already in Boston, as by this date each company on overseas service was allowed to take six wives.

On 20 May Pitcairn decided to form his marines into battalions as this was 'necessary for the good of the service': when the rest of the reinforcements landed on 24 May the 1st and 2nd Marine Battalions were formed. Each commanded by a major – Major James Short the 1st, Maj John Tupper the 2nd – with a small staff, and the 'flank' companies of grenadiers and light infantry selected from volunteers. One grenadier and one light company served in each battalion with eight battalion companies, 20 companies in all. They lived in tented camps and their captains were 'to pay their companies in the same manner practised by land forces'.

The month before the marine reinforcements landed, the Massachusetts Committee of Public Safety (a revolutionary or Whig body) had called out the militia the day after the withdrawal from Lexington (20 April). These forces blocked the landward approaches to Boston, but the British navy controlled Massachusetts Bay and its islands were used to grow hay for the British army's horses and for stores dumps. On Noodles Island, east of Charlestown and only 400m from the Bay's north shore, some 300 cattle and milking cows were grazed until a raiding force of 200 Americans started to drive them off on the morning of 27 May. The schooner HMS *Diana* landed 40 Marines and in attempting to give them covering fire with her swivel guns, she went aground. A further 80 Marines were landed with two 3-pounders, HMS *Britannia* coming inshore to support them. She was forced to withdraw, however, after being holed by the Americans' cannon fire and after 11 hours of skirmishing the Marines were withdrawn. That night the Americans destroyed naval stores they could not take away from the island; and having stripped *Diana* of 'anything that might be useful' – some of her guns later proving extremely so – she was burnt. A direct result of this raid was a severe milk shortage, for 'regiments [which] had cows distributed to them [were] requested to send "what milk they can spare" to the general Hospital'.

By mid-June the Massachusetts Provincial Congress were raising an army of 30,000, half from the Bay area who were to receive coats on enlistment and half from other New England states. Among these were a few experienced Indian fighters, who had served the British with Rogers' Rangers fighting the French 20 years earlier. Many were local farmers, others were youngsters who had never shot anything larger than a squirrel and had to be shown the weight of shot and powder needed to kill a man. Nearly all wore their homespun clothes, the officers wearing a simple sash of office if they had any distinguishing mark of dress at all. At Bunker Hill they would be under the nominal command of the former Ranger and by now prosperous Col Israel Putman, a short square-jawed 57-year-old.

A force of 1,200 were sent on Friday night, 16 June, to fortify Bunker Hill but instead built defences on Breed's Hill a mere 20m high, against the more commanding 35m of the first choice, from where batteries would have been better placed to fire across the narrows of the harbour entrance. From the main redoubt a breastwork ran 100m northward, beyond this – the gap covered by three v-shaped outposts – ran the fence. This was a stone wall surmounted by two rails, against which a second fence was later laid with loose straw between the two, appearing as a solid obstacle to the eye although not musket-ball proof. The line of this 'fence' went northward for 300m to the shore of the Mystic River. At least five cannon were installed in the defences, with five iron swivel-guns from *Diana* spaced along the fence.

To the south men would take positions in the houses of Charlestown overlooking the easterly approach of farm land interspersed with marsh to Breed's Hill. 'A slight defence of stones' was also built where the fence came down to the shore of the Mystic River. Although described as 'slight', Col John Stark – a one-time Ranger and experienced Indian fighter – saw that the fence might be outflanked.

He had built this stone defence-work above the 8-ft (2+m) bluff near the water's edge, keeping the best of his New Hampshire Regiment to man it.

These defences forestalled Gen Gage's plans to fortify Bunker Hill and the Dorchester Heights, the Americans having heard of his plans three days earlier. However, the first reports of the activity above Charlestown, only reached the British commander at dawn (4 am) on Saturday. Before then HMS *Lively* began bombarding Breed's Hill but to little effect, although later that day the British ships' bombardment of Charlestown Neck would be a decisive factor for it discouraged many militia regiments joining those in the defences, after a steady stream of American reinforcements crossed the Charlestown Neck early in the day, 800 men joining those building the defences. Gen Gage, realising the dangers if batteries were installed on these hills, ordered 20 flank companies drawn from his most seasoned regiments – including those of the 2nd Marines – to parade at 11.30 am. By this time cooks had prepared three days' cooked rations for each man, which should not go bad in the summer heat when carried with his ammunition, a blanket and pack. The practice of deploying flank companies from each regiment as storm troops was not unusual at that time, regiments were administrative rather than tactical formations. This practice with flank companies also ensured that the best troops were on the flanks ready to exploit success or protect the less experienced men in battalion companies from flank attacks by cavalry.

In Boston the 20 flank companies with the other companies of 5th and 38th Regiments (1,500 in all) embarked in ships' boats from the Long Wharf out of shot, if not sight, of the Americans on Breed's Hill. They would be rowed 2.4km to land on the eastern tip of the Charlestown peninsula, some 550m from the redoubt, while ships and Copp's battery bombarded it. There was also some cover from a small hill near this beach. A second

The Battle of Bunker Hill 1775

force – some flank companies, 52nd and 43rd Regiments – were ready to embark at North Battery, 800m nearer the landing beaches. Here also the 1st Marines and 47th Regiment were drawn up as a third force ready to follow the second.

Gen Howe, Gage's second-in-command, with Brig-Gen Pigot landed with the 20 flank companies, his men getting ashore without interference while British ships bombarded the redoubt. He made the customary senior officers' reconnaissance, and decided to bring over his second force of 1,000 men in six flank companies, the 52nd and 43rd Regiments. They landed unscathed although the tide was

The British initially landed most of their army on the eastern tip of the Charlestown peninsular and made two assaults. When these failed to break into the American redoubt on Breed's Hill more troops, including Marines who had landed nearer the town, were brought into the third attack which cleared the redoubt. This diagram outlines these actions, fought on 17 June 1775.

ebbing, which forced the supporting ships *Glasgow* and *Somerset* (68 guns) to move further off shore and prevented some batteries on rafts coming inshore further west, where they might have strengthened the bombardment of the Rebels' lines of communication across Charlestown Neck. Nor, at this state of tide, could a landing be made to the west or north-west in the rear of the American defences, for the ebb was too strong.

The General divided his two forces into three columns: the grenadiers on the left would advance some 550m to attack the redoubt; in the centre the battalion companies would attack the breastwork and fence; on the right 11 light companies would move along the north shore to outflank the defences. That at least was the broad plan. The opening rounds, however, were not auspicious for the 6-pounder field guns sent forward to bombard the defences had 12-pound shot in error as their reserves, nor could they cross marshy ground to get near enough to fire grape.

As the grenadiers' column marched forward they had to cross the back of Charlestown, and were cut down by withering fire from the houses. They were checked and in the knee-high grass, crossing fences and some stone walls, their attempts to form a line was fragmented. The battalion companies were also stopped, for although the Americans in the redoubt had not fired earlier – waiting to aim low when 'the handsome coats [of officers] can be clearly seen' – they now took a heavy toll of British officers. Some were hit by 'chewed bullets' (no doubt nicked by a knife) that splayed out like dumdum bullets, tearing great holes in the flesh. One American marksman, bravely standing a metre clear of the redoubt, fired shot after shot as loaded muskets or rifles were passed up to him. He had picked off some 20 officers before he was killed by fire from the grenadiers.

As his field guns could not range, Gen Howe sent a boat across to Copp's Hill battery, opposite Charlestown, where an

additional six 24-pounders had been installed by seamen and Marines although now manned by army gunners. They 'threw a parcel of shells (hot shot and carcasse) and the whole of Charlestown was instantly ablaze'.

On the British right the swivel guns and accurate musket fire by John Stark's men prevented the light companies outflanking the defence. Therefore Howe rallied his men for a second attack, 15 minutes after the first. The men, still carrying their packs despite the oppressive heat and short of officers, nevertheless advanced. Again accurate fire from the redoubt held them and they fell back to the foot of Breed's Hill. Meanwhile the 1st Marines, 47th Regiment and another six flank companies had landed 'close under Charlestown just east of the blazing houses. The wooden church steeples burned in pyramids of fire, ships in stocks under repair toppled and burnt, whole streets falling together in ruins', as the tinder-dry wooden houses burst into flames. The heat from these fires adding to the warmth of that summer's day, the soldiers who had survived the first two attempts on the redoubt slipped off their packs and lay in the long grass.

They had been fighting for some two hours and it was now mid-afternoon, as the column in 'fours' of Marines and the 47th marched towards the foot of the hill. The Marines were in the van, their colours flying, with Maj Pitcairn at their head. They advanced with measured pace for in this third attack Howe concentrated his forces against the redoubt, while making only a feint at the fence. The Marines formed line with the 47th in line behind them, as these lines moved forward behind the remnants of grenadiers and regiments who had made the earlier attacks. Smoke from the burning houses stung their eyes and the menacing silence from the redoubt, like the quiet before a storm, was full of foreboding for men who had seen nearly 1,000 killed or wounded in the last hour.

The Marines fixed bayonets but as the

lines moved forward they became broken in crossing fences, stumbling to keep up in the knee-high grass, and struggling across stone walls. The leading companies faltered and the Marines passed through with Majors Pitcairn, Short and Tupper each leading the companies forward until 'immediately under the work (redoubt) we were checked' their Adjutant, Lt John Waller, later wrote. 'In confusion after being broken several times (in crossing rail fences) . . . had we stopped there much longer, the enemy would have picked us all off'. Maj Pitcairn seeing that to charge the redoubt was their only hope, sent his adjutant to ask the colonel of the 47th to form up on the Marines' left, while the adjutant ran to the Marine companies to tell them to hold their fire as the 47th moved into position.

'When we had got in tolerable order, we rushed on, leaped the ditch and climbed the parapet, under a most sore and heavy fire'. In this Maj Pitcairn was mortally wounded, before the Marines, tumbling over dead bodies, followed the Americans, who were running short of ammunition and had been ordered to fall back along the line of the fence. Some Americans were killed in the hand-to-hand fighting, using their muskets as clubs for few had bayonets, others threw rocks at the Marines before dashing for the cover of the fence. The light companies (in short coats with pockets added for ball and flints) were sent after them. But they took heavy casualties from the swivel guns and the Americans' musket fire from the natural cover these farmers and woodsmen used to great advantage. John Waller's Marines, should perhaps not have stopped against orders, to fire at the redoubt, but advanced steadily 'Now for the glory of the marines' as Maj Pitcairn commanded. Nevertheless they had been among the first into the redoubt, wielding 15 pounds of musket with its 14-inch bayonet, although John Waller later described their bayonet work as 'shocking' by good drill standards.

The redoubt had fallen at about 4 o'clock, it was 45 yards square and almost invulnerable to cannon. Half an hour afterwards there were still Americans on the battle field. Two of them, not prepared to surrender, shot an aged lieutenant of the 38th as he was changing his socks. Maj Pitcairn died after being evacuated to Boston, Maj Short had been killed as had several officers of the 2nd Marines' grenadier and light companies. In all seven marine officers and 22 rank-and-file were killed or died of wounds, including Lt Richard Shed in his mid-50s, whose son was also serving in America, and who had seen service with a Marine Regiment in 1745. The total British casualties were about 1,100 of which about a quarter were killed; considerably less were the 441 American casualties, although throughout the battle British ships had bombarded the defences, albeit from some distance at low tide, and as the Americans withdrew they again came under fire crossing Charlestown Neck.

About half the Americans on the peninsula had been in action at any one time, with little more than 3,000 Americans in all and 3,500 British of which only 400 took part in the last attack, for – as we will see in a moment – the size of companies, battalions and regiments was considerably smaller than these units in modern times. Nevertheless, having inflicted losses on the British, in what they regarded as a moral victory over regular troops, the American militia became dangerously over-confident. They had not realised the valuable part played by officers like the former Rangers Israel Putman and John Stark who had considerable military experience. To this they blended an understanding of their militiamen's limitations in a remarkable example of good leadership.

Col Tooker Collins, who had fought at Belle Isle, was sent from Plymouth to command the 2nd Marines who were brought back to Boston a few days after the battle. The 1st Marines remained on the Charlestown peninsula, encamped on

The siege of Charleston, South Carolina was one of many actions in the American War of Independence. A British army of 8,700 with 5,000 seamen and Marines had sailed in December 1779 to capture the town but were unable to begin a siege until April 1780, the fleet having been scattered by gales. The Americans blocked the channel across the bar 5km south-east of the town but British ships were lightened to cross into the Cooper estuary and 500 seamen and Marines landed on its east bank. Meanwhile the siege lines (see map) were pushed closer to the American defences, and 200 seamen and Marines captured a redoubt on Sullivan's Island where Fort Moultrie overlooked the bar and the fort surrendered to an Army force. By 11 May the British were firing hot-shot into the town which surrendered next day. There were 2,650 soldiers of the American Continental Army taken prisoner together with many armed civilians.

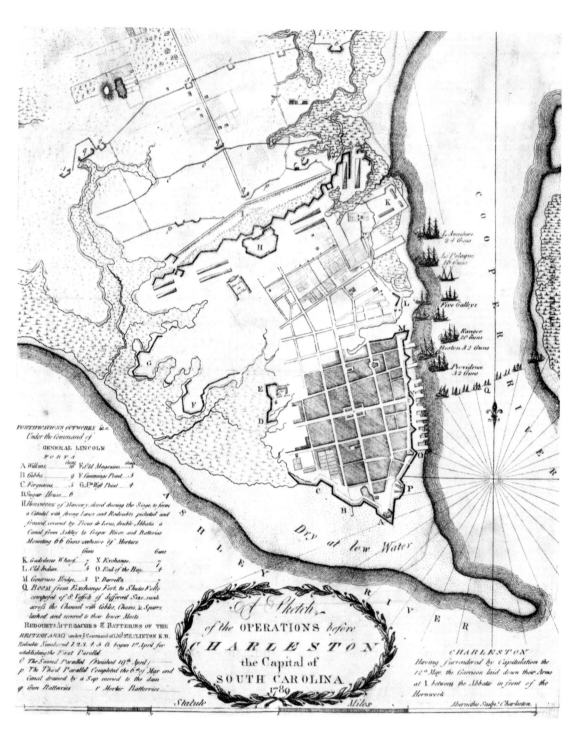

Bunker's hill where there was several feet of snow in an exceptionally bad winter. Before then there would be skirmishes with the Americans, the 2nd Marines being complimented for holding their fire and not wasting ammunition as Americans moved beyond range.

At other times these probes came closer and two Marines were captured in a skirmish on Charlestown Neck where American and British trenches came close to each other. Thirty more were surprised and their officer killed when 200 Americans raided Great Brewster Island to destroy its lighthouse. Americans fortified the Dorchester Heights, seized supply ships, burnt the garrison's haystacks on an island, and tightened their investment of the town. Reinforcements were then drawn from Fleet Marines to replace casualties and a few deserters. Several Marines are known to have come from New England and they, understandably, had sympathy with the Rebels. Many British consciences were also troubled by the conflict, Capt James Wilson a Member of Parliament resigning his commission in the Marines because he could not 'consistently with his conscience . . . continue to serve'. A corporal from the *Lively* deserted and was appointed a captain and adjutant in the American militia. The war, indeed, had many elements akin to civil war.

The reorganised Marine battalions were short of some junior officers but rebuilt the strength of the 20 companies each of some 58 all ranks, their strength before Bunker Hill. While in Boston the army regiments were each 300 to 450 strong, although their establishment was 728. The Marines would serve in Boston until the withdrawal to Quebec the following spring, after Boston had been heavily bombarded from Dorchester Heights and Phipps farm batteries. An amphibious attack on the former had to be cancelled due to rough weather on 5 March and five days later the embarkation began. This took a week to complete as 9,000 troops (some sources suggest more) and 1,500 Tory Bostonians (i.e. loyalists) were loaded into ships, with the Marines spread in detachments throughout the fleet 'to assist in the navigation'. Their departure was watched by 25,000 Americans who did not interfere, as the British had agreed not to burn the town. Although the transports sailed on 17 March they anchored in Nantasket Roads 8km south of the town for 10 days before sailing for Quebec.

The war with America continued for another seven years, the Marines (albeit as one battalion from April 1777) serving at Quebec, on Long Island (August 1776) at Philadelphia (September 1777) and elsewhere before the peace treaty of 1783. By then France, the most powerful nation in Europe, had been allies of the Americans for nearly five years, and on their

A typical young Marine officer of the time: Lieutenant John Hugh Griffiths when aged about 20. He joined the Corps at Chatham on 18 July 1778 and was killed on 27 January 1782 aboard HMS *Prudent*, of 64 guns, while in action against the French off St Kitts, west Indies. Engraving by V. Green.

entry into the war it became another contest of sea power, with Spain joining the French in June 1779 and the Netherlands in 1780.

Although the French fleets failed to provide the expected support for the Americans, the presence of French ships contributed to the defeat of over 8,000 British and German troops in Yorktown, Virginia during September 1781.

This loss, a quarter of the British forces in America, gives some measure of the size of forces engaged.[3] While the 20,000 Americans besieging the town had included militiamen. Some of them had been known to arrive on the morning of a battle only to leave in the afternoon, because their terms of service under their State's law had expired. In later wars the conscription of mass armies would change the nature of peoples' involvement in national wars, especially in Europe. Against these mass armies, of France especially, Britain would need allies with large populations, while she provided a powerful navy. In this the Royal Marines would form up to a quarter of the fighting personnel. (See Note 1 for summary of the actions of 1755–1815.)

Chapter 3

Sea Battles, Raids and Guerrilla Campaigns

The ships of the 18th century were surprisingly frail. Even in moderate weather the steady pounding of waves could crush the bows of the older ships, and frequently sickness reduced the strength of a crew to a dangerously small number. Ill-health often arose from the restricted diet that the seamen and Marines lived on – salt pork every Sunday and Thursday, beef every Saturday and Tuesday – which encouraged scurvy and fever. Even Capt Cook, one of the first naval officers to pay careful attention to diet, lost 30 of his 85 seamen and Marines during the two years of his first voyage of exploration in the Pacific. Five years later, in 1774–75, only four men 'died of fevers' on a similar voyage in *Resolution* and *Adventure*. It was on this voyage that Cook was killed by natives in Hawaii, despite the bravery of his small escort of Marines.

By the beginning of the 19th century the diet of the men had improved but there had been no substantial change in ship design, partly because of the length in service of each ship. HMS *Victory*, for example, was nearly 40 years old when she sailed from Portsmouth in the spring of 1803 to become Admiral Lord Nelson's flagship. Capt Charles W. Adair, the Marine detachment's commander, was a conscientious officer in his late 30s who had been commissioned for some 20 years, and had served as the Adjutant of the Marine battalion at the Cape of Good Hope in 1775 and had commanded No. 10 Chatham Company since October 1800. Adair undoubtedly commanded the respect of his men during the $2\frac{1}{2}$ years of Nelson's remorseless hunt for the French and Spanish squadrons.

Napoleon, who never seems to have understood naval strategy, had ordered squadrons to the West Indies where they were to join with Spanish ships and sweep back towards the Channel to defeat the British Western Squadron. Napoleon believed the British ships would by now be worn out from years of blockading but in this he was wrong, for in the Mediterranean Nelson, who considered 'the greatest thing in military service is health', was among the first senior naval officers to be concerned with the well-being of the lower deck ratings. When a Dr Gillespie joined *Victory* in January 1805 there was only one man in the sick bay, from her crew of 840. Many other ships' companies were equally fit, although the men seldom, if ever, went ashore except under an armed Marine guard when watering ships. Nelson himself did not put a foot on land for two years and ten days after boarding *Victory*.

In August *Victory* sailed to join Vice-Admiral Collingwood's squadron off Cadiz. Admiral Nelson was to command this fleet, but such was his reputation with the French Admirals that on 28 September, when *Victory* and two '74s' arrived, there were no gun salutes in order not to warn the French of his arrival. Nelson had always planned not just a splendid victory over the French but the annihilation of their fleet, and for this he expected to have 40 ships-of-the-line. To bring so many ships into action in the conventional line of battle would, he considered, take so long that the French would escape. Therefore he planned to attack in three squadrons, or divisions, each under a Vice-Admiral with the initiative to exploit any

break in the enemy's line. At Trafalgar this is broadly what happened, but there were only two British divisions since some ships were taking on fresh stores at Gibraltar in that third week in October.

The French Admiral's Combined Fleet of 18 French and 15 Spanish ships had spent much of the war years bottled up in port. They were not, therefore, as practised in gunnery as the British but were able to exercise in small arms and close-quarter fighting. This largely dictated their tactics, with guns fired to dismast British ships before attempting to take them by boarding.

In contrast, the British crews had been at sea for at least two years in many cases, but few ships carried a full complement. Their seamen gunners (Royal Marines would not generally be trained as gunners until 1829) were capable of firing three aimed broadsides in five minutes, and the

better trained crews achieved this in 3½ minutes. No ships could stand for long against such weights of fire; *Victory*'s double shotted broadside weighed 1.14 tonnes. There is reason to believe, though, that the penetration of shot was less than might be expected unless a ship could be raked through her less protected stern by shot travelling to her bows.

The Royal Marine detachments were employed on the poop and upper decks as sharpshooters, sometimes in the rigging (a practice of which Nelson disapproved) and were ready to repel boarders. Other Marines were stationed throughout the ship as guards on magazines. Their officers were almost invariably on the poop deck, the senior RM Officer being close enough to the ship's Captain to hear his orders. Many Marines in working the ship were as handy as sailors and retained their skills in rope work and so on which

The death of Captain James Cook RN at Kealakakua Bay, Hawaii on 14 February 1779 during his third voyage of exploration in the Pacific. He had landed with a Marine guard of Lieutenant Molesworth Phillips and four men. The lieutenant protected Cook for as long as he could from the hostile Hawaiians; the Marines were clubbed to death, Cook was stabbed as he called to the boats' crews to hold their fire, and only Phillips escaped back to the ship (this painting by Webber mistakenly shows two men swimming to safety). Dixson Galleries, Sydney.

G. R.

Royal Marines.
WANTED,
A few young Men and Lads to complete the above distinguished Corps.

Young Men defirous of enroling themfelves will receive the
HIGHEST BOUNTIES AND EVERY ENCOURAGEMENT.

The *Advantages* of ferving in this *old eftablifhed Corps* are generally known: while on Shore they are ftationed in comfortable Barracks, on board Ship they have the *fame Allowances* as the *Navy;* befides their Pay they receive one pound of the beft Beef, one ditto of Bread, Flour, Butter, Cheefe, Tea, Sugar, &c. and a pint of the beft Wine, or half a pint of the *ftrongeft* Brandy or *Rum*. They likewife fhare in *Prize Money* with the *Navy*, by which *thoufands* have acquired *confiderable Fortunes*, and are enabled to return to their Friends in *Comfort* and *Independence*.

In Addition to the above Advantages, when embarked they can allot half of their Pay to their Wives or Relations, which will be paid them by the Collectors at their Places of Refidence.

Young Men or Lads, wifhing to enter into the ROYAL MARINES, will meet with the moft kind and honourable Treatment, by applying at the

ROYAL MARINE RENDEZVOUS,
Square & Compasses, Dale-street, Liverpool;

N. B. Such Recruits as can write and behave well, will be fure of Promotion.

A School Mafter is appointed to inftruct thofe who wifh to poffefs the great Advantages of Learning.

BRINGERS OF GOOD RECRUITS WILL RECEIVE THREE GUINEAS.
GOD SAVE THE KING.

T. KAYE, Printer to his Royal Highnefs the DUKE of GLOUCESTER and EDINBURGH.

A recruiting poster *c.* 1802 describes the advantages of service in the Corps including a 'share in prize money with the Navy' and a daily ration of 'a pint of the best wine or half a pint of the strongest brandy or rum'.

probably enabled them to be used as general handymen about a ship.

Since the 1790s, when their loyalty was proven during the naval mutinies,[1] they had – and had until recent times – their messes placed between the officers' quarters and those of the seamen. The latter, often pressed men who might have been brought aboard a ship in 1803 not to see their homes again for 10 years, made up half of *Victory*'s crew, which also included 12% who were sent to sea by magistrates as a punishment for civilian crimes, some 60 men were foreigners. These included an Italian and a German in the RM detachment, but most of the Marines and nearly 200 of the seamen had joined for the bounty (a Marine received £17 [over nine

months pay] when he volunteered in 1804) and the attraction of prize money. Some, however, had been serving in the militia on home defence, and were encouraged by the British Government to transfer to line regiments or the Royal Marines. Two brothers from Street in Somerset enlisted with two cousins on the same day in spring 1805, and as trained militiamen were sent not to barracks but to *Achilles*' detachment in which they were to serve for 10 years.

At dawn on Monday 21 October, at about 6 am, the French fleet was sailing southward 15–20km east of Nelson with Cape Trafalgar some 18km further east. The breeze was light, and Nelson feared that he might not bring the French to action before the afternoon, leaving too few hours of autumn daylight in which to destroy them, even if the French had not turned earlier for the safety of Cadiz. At 6.40 am he signalled the fleet to form two columns: the Windward Column was led by Nelson in *Victory* and the Leeward Column was led by Collingwood in *Royal Sovereign*. Shortly afterwards *Victory* signalled 'Prepare for battle'. Royal Marines checked their muskets. Ball and powder was issued and probably reserves of ammunition brought up and secured in chests on gratings near the mizzen and main masts. The Marines were dressed in working rig: 'in their check shirts and blue trousers there was no distinguishing Marine from seaman'. All would 'work like horses', while the geese for the Captain's table fluttered and honked in their slate-sided crates below decks. There are few records of detachment actions during the coming battle, emphasising the extent to which the Royal Marine involvement was essentially the same as that of each ship's company.

At 8 am the Combined Fleet was seen to begin to turn into the wind onto a northerly course, for Admiral Villeneuve feared that he would be cut off from Cadiz. In the failing breeze some ships had to put boats over the side to tow them round. The manoeuvre took two hours,

leaving them in a long crescent with many ships to lee of the line, which in places became 'double-banked'. *Victory*, meanwhile, having ordered a change of course to 'Easterly', signalled 'make all sail possible with safety to masts'. Nevertheless she could only plough on at a slow walking-pace of three knots, falling to as little as $1\frac{1}{2}$ knots despite her great spread of canvas: her main mast, 'three houses high' was over 60m (203ft) above the waterline, making an impressive sight for the 40 Marines drawn up probably in two ranks on either side of the poop deck.

Collingwood's *Royal Sovereign*, newly copper-bottomed so she was not slowed by weed fouling, outsailed the other ships in the Lee Column. She passed into the Combined Fleet's crescent line to fire her first broadside into the Spanish 112-gun *Santa Ana* and for the next 10 minutes or more was alone engaging five ships. *Belle Isle* came up, a taut silence in the ship, interrupted only by the Captain's orders, 'Steady! Starboard a little, steady so'. This was echoed by the Master directing the helmsman, as shots passed over the ship. 'A shriek soon followed – a cry of agony was produced by the next shot' as this caught one of the 30 Marines on *Belle Isle*'s poop. The next shot decapitated another Marine and the bloodshed would get heavier as *Belle Isle* passed astern of *Royal Sovereign* to engage two ships. *Victory* leading the Weather Column was nearing her first opponent about then.

The Recruit for the Corps in about 1805. Edward Bird, the artist, always painted from life so this is almost certainly an actual Marine sergeant of the time acting as a recruiting officer. Castle Museum, Nottingham.

The French two-decker *Redoubtable* caught between HMS *Victory* (left) and *Téméraire* (right) at about 1.40 pm in the Battle of Trafalgar. The French put up a stout resistance and attempted to board *Victory*, but were repulsed by her seamen and Marines and by broadsides from *Téméraire*. Painting by A. E. F. Mayer; Musée de la Marine, Paris.

A seaman tossed buckets of water over the canvas covers to the hammocks, stowed in nets along the decks to give some protection from musket fire. He splashed some water on the uniform of a young Marine officer and was cursed for his carelessness. Nelson, always mindful of the lower deck's interest, overheard these words, and told the young officer it was his own fault 'and wished he'd had the whole bucket full'. The Admiral saw the first shots fall short of *Victory*, but

more followed, one going through the main topgallant sail. The French Admiral Villeneuve's flagship, the 80-gun *Bucentaure* had opened the firing. For *Victory* the approach was a most dangerous tactic, as the Column formed the perpendicular of a letter 'T' which the French crossed. They could fire broadsides into *Victory* but she had virtually no guns that would bear on them. At 500m, *Bucentaure*'s fire carried away *Victory*'s mizzen top mast, and another shot smashed her pair of

The Battle of Trafalgar. The British columns' attacks on the Combined French–Spanish Fleet showing positions just before noon on 21 October 1805. There were 2,700 Royal Marine officers and men serving in the British ships in this action.

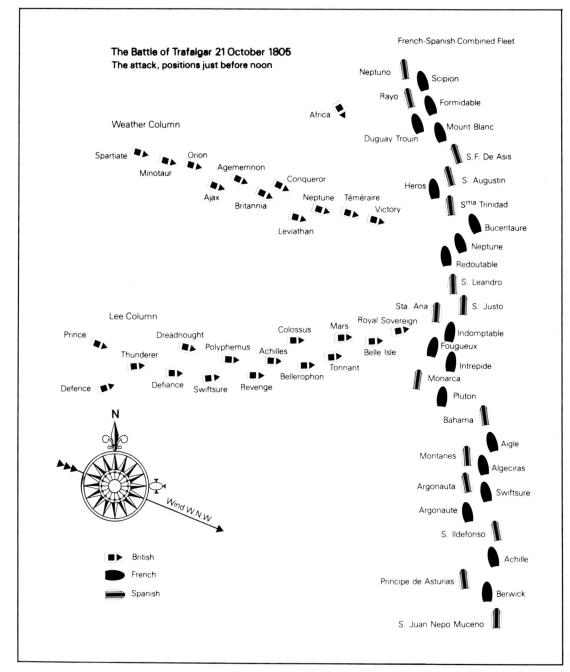

2-m (5ft 9ins) wheels. Minutes later a vicious double-headed shot smashed along the poop, cutting down eight Marines as they stood in close formation, muskets ready but out of range of their targets. Nelson himself then told Capt Adair to disperse his men under the protection of hammock-filled netting.

Meanwhile *Téméraire*, sailing first on *Victory*'s port quarter, would later pass under *Victory*'s stern, for the Admiral, clearly bent on his declared aim of a hero's death and burial in Westminster Abbey, forged ahead.

The first part of the battle, as the British ships drove pell-mell – if slowly – towards the Combined Fleet, was coming to a close. The French and Spanish ships began to close up, having seen *Royal Sovereign* break their line.

Through the smoke surrounding *Bucentaure* it was hard to make out which ships were firing, but as she cleared the bows of *Victory*, *Redoutable* could be seen closing up on her flagship, with *Neptune* further down wind. The next minute *Victory* was gliding past *Bucentaure*'s stern and discharged the port hand bow carronade into the two-decker at extremely close range.

Marines were now finding targets for from high on the three-decker's poop they overlooked the French two-deckers. Well-aimed shots at gun crews on a French quarterdeck or at their sharpshooters in the rigging, had their effect. But it would be some hours before, as one Marine claimed, 'I remained firing till there was not a man to be seen in the top'. *Victory*, drifting clear of *Bucentaure*, was next taken under fire by the 80-gun *Neptune* before this French ship ran up her jib to range ahead clear of *Victory*'s possible boarders.

Redoutable was *Victory*'s main target. Her French Captain had one of the best-

The Death of Nelson shows the moment after he was struck by a sharpshooter's bullet and Sergeant Secker RM moves to help him. The exposed decks of *Victory* were cleared almost completely of seamen gunners and Marines during the next half hour as accurate fire from *Redoubtable*'s snipers took its toll. Many if not all the Marines were dressed in the same rig as the seamen although shown here in their red coats. Painting by D. Dighton, National Maritime Museum, London.

trained crews of boarders in the Combined Fleet. His sharpshooters aloft in the rigging, where there were also small brass mortars, could also support these boarding parties by clearing an enemy's open decks, and they now poured steady fire onto *Victory*'s poop and quarter decks. One Marine, in these exposed deck positions, had become fast in rigging brought down round his ears. As he struggled to free himself from the tangle of ropes, Nelson saw his plight and taking a clasp knife from his pocket threw it to the Marine, who then cut himself free. Another Marine, his left arm smashed by a musket ball, steadied himself and 'fired his piece' at a French seaman. Satisfied no shot was wasted, the Marine then went below still carrying his musket, where his wound was cleaned up.

As *Victory*'s helm was swung to port – she was being steered from the tiller flat – her anchor stowed outboard, caught in *Redoutable*'s anchor. The two ships then fell alongside each other. The French ship's boarders, poised at their gangway to scramble up *Victory*'s starboard side, were cleared in one devastating hail of musket balls fired from *Victory*'s starboard carronade. *Victory* had been in close action for about 25 minutes when, at 1.25 pm, Admiral Nelson was hit in the left shoulder, fell forward onto his knees before collapsing on the deck, 'my backbone is shot through' he said quietly, and had his face covered so that the men would not see who Sergeant Secker and two Marines were carrying below deck. Firing continued albeit less briskly on the quarterdeck, as Marine and French casualties mounted, with probably half the Marines who had provided the deck guard dead or wounded. Some ten minutes after Nelson was shot, Jean Lucas, the French Captain of the *Redoutable*, again prepared to board *Victory*. But following *Victory* into the Combined Fleet line was *Téméraire* under Capt S. Busigny; he had come under *Victory*'s stern and now on her starboard quarter had the stud sails cut away in case he lost contact by outsailing the damaged

flagship. As Busigny put his ship further to starboard, she was heavily raked from stem to stern by broadsides from *Neptune*, a French '80'. This so damaged *Téméraire*'s masts and rigging that she was almost unmanageable and for the moment she could not assist *Victory*.

Capt Charles Adair, hearing trumpets sound from *Redoutable*, saw the dangers of an imminent boarding by the French. Already four of these brave fellows were beginning to climb across *Victory*'s anchor from their bow some 4m below *Victory*'s. Adair shouted for his men, the judder and jar, the whirls of smoke, the crash and roar of close action engulfing his words. But Adair by gesture and the help of Lt Roteley gathered men from the guns below. He then climbed the rail by the forward gangway and encouraged his seamen and Marines from this vantage point to such effect that the French were checked before Adair was killed. Then his men drove the enemy back on to *Redoutable*, an action in which *Victory* lost 18 killed and over 20 wounded.

The French were preparing to make a second determined climb into *Victory* when *Téméraire* raked the '74' with a broadside that killed or wounded 200 including Jean Lucas. Although wounded he remained on deck, fighting his ship for another 15 minutes before she was overwhelmed, although she did not completely surrender. During this time, while this French '74' was sandwiched between the two British three-deckers, a Corporal – the stump of one arm bound up in Adair's discarded sash – led eight men across the gap into *Redoutable*, although records show that she did not finally strike her colours until 2.20 pm and then to *Téméraire*. *Victory*, before then, was manoeuvring herself (or trying to do so) clear of the tangle of ships.

Victory, her sails tattered and masts sorely gashed, finally succeeded with her fire-booms in getting free of *Redoutable* at about 2.00 pm. The second phase of the battle had begun, with a rough and tumble melée of ship-to-ship actions, rather than

fire fights between formed squadrons. So far, in Collingwood's words, it had been 'a severe action – no dodging or man-oeuvering'.

At about 4.45 pm Admiral Nelson died satisfied, 'I have done my duty; I praise God for it'. His body was preserved in rum in a cask to be carried home for burial, but for the others the eternal battle against the sea would continue. The dead were fetched from the surgeon's space in the cockpit of each ship, many having died from loss of blood while waiting for attention: 'For the rule is, as order is requisite, that every man shall be dressed in rotation as they are brought down wounded'. The corpses were thrown over the side. Jury rigs were lashed up on *Victory* and other ships, and tangles of rigging cut away with axes, where these spars could not be salvaged. There was a call about 5.30 pm in most ships, for 'all hands to splice the main brace' and a gill

(one-tenth litre) of rum was issued to every man, they also had their first meal since breakfast. Around this time the French '74' *Achille* blew up. The reverber-ations of her explosion finally ended the battle.

The story of Royal Marines at Trafalgar is the story of the ships in which they served. On these occasions, the individu-al's self-reliance and initiative has much in common with commandos of the 1980s. In a typical incident two of the Marines from the five men of the prize-crew aboard the French flagship guarded her maga-zines below deck from the several hun-dred Frenchmen; one Marine in another prize crew was shot by a dying seaman; two of the many incidents after British ships had cut the French line, which we can now follow.

Royal Sovereign's battle developed into a slogging match with the Admiral Alva's flag ship, the 130-gun *Santa Ana*. After

A cutting-out action. On the night of 22–23 July 1801 seamen and Marines successfully boarded the 20-gun French corvette *Chevrette*, which carried a reinforced crew of 339 seamen and soldiers who had loaded her guns to the muzzles with grapeshot. The British lost 12 killed (including Lt James Sinclair of the Marines) and 57 wounded from the 180 men in ten boats who had carried through this action, but nevertheless captured *Chevrette* and sailed her out of Camaret Bay (near St Tropez). Painting by P. J. de Loutherbourg, City Art Gallery, Bristol.

some two hours this Spanish ship was 'nearly beaten in' and she struck at 2.15 pm, her Admiral dangerously wounded and many of the crew dead. *Royal Sovereign* had 141 killed and wounded including her senior Marine 1st lieutenant and 29 of his men. The heaviest losses in both the Weather and Lee Columns fell to their leading ships; and there is an argument for saying that Nelson fought the battle with only two-thirds of his fleet as some of his slowest ships did not break into the enemy line until 3 pm, nearly three hours after the first engagement.

Belle Isle, a '74' (two-decker) having been engaged by some six ships, nevertheless about 1.25 pm sent her last serviceable boat away with a prize crew to *Argonaute*. An hour later the '74' lost her foremast and by mid-afternoon was a hulk, using sweep oars through the gun ports to bring 'our battery towards the enemy' with Marines from the poop helping to serve guns on her quarterdeck. *Tonnant* (an '80') had cut the line some quarter of an hour after *Belle Isle*. The '80' became so closely engaged with the *Algeciras* that the British had their 'fire-engine' playing on her broadside to put out the fire caused by the flame of our guns'. *Algeciras* at one stage put her bowsprit into the '80's' main shrouds, 'with the greater part of her officers and ship's company ready to board *Tonnant*'. But her Marines killed many Frenchmen by accurate fire, while the forecastle gun loaded with grape was manhandled to aim into the enemy bowsprit. The boarders were repelled.

Capt J. Wemyss RM had his detachment on one of the smallest of the '74's', *Bellerophon*. She had been engaged by four French '74s' and *Aigle* causing explosions of loose powder. James Wemyss passed the First Lieutenant on the quarterdeck ladder, and in answer to the latter's concern over the Marine's wounds, replied: 'Tis only a scratch . . . I shall have to apologise . . . bye and bye for quitting the deck'. Yet John Wemyss had eight musket balls in his body and was going

below to have an arm amputated, an operation which proved fatal. The highest casualties among seamen and marines were aboard *Collossus* a '74'. In a two-hour fight she overcame two '74s' but paid the price of 200 killed and wounded including her Captain. He was killed and among the wounded were 40 Marines, over half of her detachment.

The efficient musketry of the *Leviathan*'s Marines 'swept everyone off the upper deck of *San Augustin*' and she was taken in half an hour, the Marines in the boarding parties losing two killed and four injured. On *Revenge* (a '74') Marines again shot Spaniards out of the bowsprit of the three-decker *Principe de Asturias* as she tried to put them aboard 'but they caught a Tartar . . . (and) were glad to sheer off' after *Revenge* had also fired her carronade into the Spanish boarders. *Conqueror* took *Bucentaure* when Admiral Villeneuve struck his colours a little after 2 o'clock. Capt Atcherley RM with a Corporal, two Marines and two seamen were sent away in a boat to take the Admiral's formal surrender. When aboard the French flagship, Atcherley decided he should take the Admiral with his two naval captains back to *Conqueror* to surrender their swords. Leaving the two marines on *Bucentaure* as guards, the surrender party rowed to *Mars*, for *Conqueror* had sailed in search of further prizes. The Admiral was later brought aboard *Victory* at 5 pm where a Royal Marines' guard was paraded to receive him. Their best uniforms, normally kept in a locked store, had been brought out for the occasion.

Throughout the action frigates – with their relatively few guns on one deck – had provided some communication between ships-of-the-line. Collingwood, for instance, transferred his flag from the *Royal Sovereign* to the *Euryalus* (a '38') to have mobility in drawing his fleet together after the battle. But during the action, these and other small ships like the 10-gun schooner HMS *Pickle*, were seldom fired on; and there were no casualties among Marine detachments in the frigates.

The Combined Fleet with strength of over 31,000 manning 2,626 guns, had suffered nearly 8,000 casualties and 7,000 taken prisoner. Their loss of ships (22 from the 33 which sailed on 20 October) was devastating. The British lost 449 killed and 1,241 wounded from crews totalling probably no more than 16,800 all hands. Of the 2,700 Marines, 117 had been killed and 219 wounded. Those survivors who had been wounded received awards of from £10 to £50 according to their rank and the severity of their wound.

The Napoleonic Wars continued for another decade, during which time RM Artillery gunners manned mortars and bomb vessels, known as 'bombs'. They fired rockets from oared launches and experimented with early types of torpedoes in raids across the Channel. More conventional, although no less difficult raids, were made by Fleet Marines against French strongholds on the Spanish coast. At Roasa, some 25km from Spain's northeast border, 5,000 French troops surrounded the town in November 1808. The inhabitants fled but the Citadel and the principal outwork of the defences, the tower-fort Trinidad, were both held. Their Spanish garrisons (here allies of England) were reinforced by seamen and Marines, Lt Thomas How RM taking 25 Marines to the fort. There they and later two reinforcements each of 30 Marines with 30 seamen, withstood repeated French attacks for three weeks before being withdrawn. The following year Napoleon led his army to victory in Spain, forcing Wellington to withdraw to Portugal behind the defence works of Torres Vedras. These stretched 50km from the sea to the Tagus, 45km north of Lisbon.

In April 1810 RMA companies were ordered to Cadiz where they joined over 3,500 British and Portuguese troops helping the Spanish garrison. They had been under siege since mid-February, the French building batteries to bombard the harbour. These had not been completed, however, before the first three bombs

vessels arrived to 'shell' French working parties. Later the French brought up 12 *Villantroys*, howitzer-mortars, cast in Seville; but in order to get the weight of shell for the 6,000m range, these 'howitzer' shells were partly filled with lead and as a result did little damage when first fired on 31 December.

More effective with the limited power of weapons at this time was the small-scale raid to blow-up a fort, make a road impassable to carts, the cutting out of troublesome privateers, or landing guerrillas as Commodore Pophams's squadron did the previous July. He put ashore 1,000 men from the large force of irregulars operating in the Asturian mountains (north Spain), and after this landing on the Basque coast, they raided Santona near Santander. Other landings were supported by this squadron, while in the south seamen and Marines from Gibraltar were raiding French strong points. Typically, on the night of 28 September 1810 the 14-gun sloop *Rambler* sent boats to reconnoitre the mouth of the Barbate river, west of Cape Trafalgar. Thirty seamen and Marines led by Lt James Seagrave RN and Lt William Halstead RM – who had experience of raids on the Albanian coast – rowed into the anchorage to find a privateer. Her crew were ashore guarding the river bank, with 30 French Dragoons and two 6-pounders. The raiders landed, attacking this party with such fury that seven men and seven horses were killed, the rest then withdrew in some confusion in the dark. Men from the landing party swam out to the privateer, clambered up her anchor chains and 'carried her' to use a phrase of those times.

Maj Richard Williams RMA, commanding 1st RM Battalion, landed in Spain in December 1810. The battalion served in the lines of Torres Vedras until 16 January, their RMA company manning Army guns across the river Tagus from Lisbon at Fort Almada. This battalion was re-equipped in Portsmouth during the spring and returned to Spain as a Strike Force in Commodore Popham's Flying Squadron.

Their transport, the *Diadem*, if not exactly a Commando ship, was a converted '64' which had been trooping since 1798. At 160ft (50 + m) with a 44½-ft beam, she had carried almost 700 Marines, six companies of the battalion with an RMA company of 53 all ranks, for the men to be transferred to other ships as operations required. This battalion of picked men were in many ways an élite of élites, newly kitted out; they had a full establishment of ordnance stores and pioneer equipment including entrenching tools, scaling ladders, 1,000 sand bags, petards (demolition charges), a portable forge and an armourer's chest of tools. Their artillery company manned two 6-pounder field guns and a 5½-in (133-mm) howitzer for which they had 50 rounds of case shot (shrapnel), with 200 similar rounds for the 6-pounders. On 16 June *Diadem* rendezvoused with the squadron off Santona, following the plan devised by Lt Col Sir Howard Douglas. A distinguished army artillery officer, he had been sent to organise guerrillas in Galicia (north-west Spain). Douglas had discussed the plan with Wellington who strongly supported its aim: to ensnare French forces in the north by aiding the guerrilla forces in these regions. A plan which would succeed to a remarkable degree.

One infantry company and the RMA company were transferred to Popham's flagship the *Venerable* ('74') and other companies to the frigates *Surveillante*, *Medusa* and *Rhine* – although why some ships carried more than a company is not clear, for the squadron also included the *Magnificent* ('74'), two more frigates as well as two brigs, a sloop and small boats.

The first action, against Lequito 65km west of San Sebastian, began with a bombardment by *Venerable*. She could not elevate her guns, however, to effectively bombard the hill fort nearby with its 100-man garrison. A 24-pounder was therefore hoisted out of the ship, loaded onto a boat or a 'flat' and towed ashore. In the heavy surf on the beach the landing was difficult but as guerrilla forces held

the ground the French could not interfere. Having reached the shore, however, the gun crews' difficulties had only just begun for a movable capstan had to be used to haul gun and cradle up the beach. The gun, nevertheless, was in position by 4 pm on a ridge overlooking the fort and in four hours breached the wall. Then, at their second attempt, a storming party of guerrillas took the fort, its garrison retreating to a large fortified convent.

This was held by another 200 Frenchmen and lay on the outskirts of the town with houses in the line of fire from the ships, but it was also overlooked by a small island some 200m from the beach. That night more Marine gunners and some infantry Marines were landed from frigates onto this island. They brought ashore three carronades but when a second 24-pounder was landed next day, the garrison (men of the 119th Regiment) surrendered. The fortifications were then blown up and their 18-pounder guns destroyed before the Squadron sailed out of the bay as 1,100 French infantry marched into the town.

The squadron made several landings in the next week, destroying batteries and coast defences, the guerrillas co-ordinating their attacks with these raids. The French, with garrisons of 300 to 1,000 infantry guarding key ports, were usually defending mediaeval castles and fortified monasteries. They had columns of all arms – cavalry, infantry and field guns – based some kilometres inland, ready to reinforce any threatened garrison. The columns, however, marching and countermarching over rough hill tracks, could not keep up with the Flying Squadron. Its feints here, then swift raid there, sometimes 80km away – not 10 hours' sailing distance – took its effect. The local Spaniards, 'raised [in] a flame of excitement' were harassing the French columns, while several thousand muskets were landed by small boats from the Squadron to arm recruits joining the guerrilla's socalled 'Seventh Army'. The French commander of their 'Army of the North' believed that a British fleet was about to land an invasion force, recalled two infantry and one cavalry division after they had started south, because, he wrote, 'not a man could be spared from northern Spain'. The strategy had worked as Wellington had believed it would, and there would be a bonus.

On 22 July *Magnificent* with the frigates *Surveillante* and *Medusa* ran in to the bay of the deep water port of Santander. By this time raids and landings were so familiar an operation for this Strike Force of 1st RM Battalion and ships of the Flying Squadron, that without being over-confident they undertook very difficult operations. The entrance to this port was protected by the strong Fort of St Ano and batteries on the opposite shore. The fort at least would have to be 'taken out' before the ships could attack the town, therefore Fleet Marines and RM companies embarked in the frigates and were landed that night with a large force of seamen. (The Fleet Marines may at this time have been formed into companies, for there is a reference to eight companies in one contemporary report). Each man carried out a check on his musket, that he had his screw driver (to tighten up his musket's mechanism), a worm (for clearing the barrel) and spare flints in good condition. He then paraded on the poop of 'his' frigate and might have been issued with a 'day's dry provisions in case of accidents'. In all, with a fusee, bayonet and equipment including $\frac{1}{2}$lb of tent pegs and 1lb (0.45kg) of pipe clay, he carried about 59lb (27kg).

The officer commanding each ship's landing party, having inspected the ranks, with officers and sergeants posted, told them 'the nature of the service they were going upon . . . so that they may be able to form immediately on their landing'. How many rounds they actually took on this night is not known, but soldiers usually carried 60 rounds, weighing nearly 10kg. Some of the RMA company landed with the seamen and Marines, taking ashore their two 6-pounder field guns and

the howitzer. Other RMA gunners landed that night with two of *Medusa*'s 24-pounders, these were installed by seamen on an islet in the harbour close to St Ano Fort.

A brigade of guerrillas, perhaps 3,000 men or more, were investing the town, but 1,600 Frenchmen behind its ramparts had kept them at bay. The British, led by W. T. Lake and Sir George Collier, both frigate captains, were ashore safely and bombardment of the fort began next day. The garrison held out, stubbornly firing back at their attackers, although apparently not able to silence the British guns effectively. These gradually broke up the fort's outer walls, with shrapnel from the howitzer preventing any attempts to temporarily patch up the breaches. After several hours' bombardment the garrison came out, fighting their way down the track some 3km into the town. They were pursued by the British, but the garrison commander made good use of the 'close nature of the ground, broken country with hedges and two stone-walled villages'. He counter-attacked his pursuers who that night were still some way from the town's ramparts. Next morning (26 July) they again advanced, this time more steadily. By the afternoon they were established on a ridge of high ground overlooking the walls when Gen Dubreton, the French Governor of the town, made a powerful sortie.

Almost all of the garrison, over 1,000 men, ignored the guerrillas to storm up the ridge towards the British positions. The garrison from the fort, who had been engaging the seamen and Marines, now joined this advance before the whole force withdrew. An attempt next day to follow them was repulsed, both frigate captains being wounded, as the French (firing from houses in the town) killed nine seamen and Marines. Capt Christopher Noble RM, who had commanded the Marine companies in these actions, was 'dangerously wounded and taken prisoner'. Although the British ships, having passed St Ano Fort in 'battle order' soon after its garrison quit two days earlier, were inside the harbour, carronading the town. However, the planned supporting attacks by Spanish irregulars had not materialised, although some came into the outskirts of the town and Lt Sturgeon RM – cut off at his post in a monastery – was rescued by them.

In the next five days the ships bombarded French positions at intervals and when on 2 August reinforcements of Spanish regulars arrived, plans were laid to attack an approaching relief column. That night before the Allied troops could be deployed, Gen Dubreton fought his way out of the town and through guerrilla positions to the south. His garrison joined a column marching to their relief, because the French were gathering many of their northern garrisons to reinforce Villa-francea, the town on which Wellington's army, after their victory at Salamanca, were now advancing. The remainder of the 1st Battalion had been in action against French columns attacking the garrison town of Castro further east, and all but two companies were brought to Santander on 4 August. They carried out further feints and raids, being joined at Santander on 14 August by the 2nd RM Battalion which had been formed in England some five weeks earlier and now joined the Flying Squadron. But already the French had withdrawn veteran troops from Spain to join the Grand Army which had crossed the Niemen River that June on its fateful advance into Russia. Yet although this army with French allies, was 430,000 strong, the French still had over 250,000 men in Spain, for warfare by this date involved mass armies. These had been unheard of before the 1790s, when 50,000 men were probably the largest army committed to one battle, and this number was rarely in the field.

Santander, Wellington's bonus from Commodore Popham's cruise, with its deep water port served as a supply base for both Spanish forces in northern Spain and Wellington's later campaigns. Powder, rations and other stores took some 10 days to reach the British besieging Burgos. These had to be carried over mountain tracks as were two naval guns which Wellington at first refused. However, they were too late to reach Burgos before Wellington lifted the siege that October to go into winter quarters. The Marines carried out further raids on the north coast and were in the force investing Santona, the 'Gibraltar of the north'. There they were joined by 200 Marines who had been in action against the Danes while defending Anholt Island in the Kattegat. The French, however, held out in Santona until after Wellington's victory the following year at Vitoria, east of the Asturias, from where he drove the French back across the Pyrenees that August. By then the Marine Battalions were fighting in America, having proved that one aspect of sea power is the effective use which could – and can – be made of amphibious raiding forces.

America, objecting to British interference with their ships trading into Europe, had declared war in June 1812. Their first foray by militiamen, however, failed in its intention to invade Canada, although later in the war they would repel British attempts to force an invasion through Fort Niagara on the Canadian border. Fleet Marines in the spring of 1813 made a number of successful coast raids, the 1st and 2nd Battalions were not so successful at first. The 1st Marines Brigaded with 300 of 102nd Regiment and 200 Canadian Chasseurs, made raids which came to grief, because the two Admirals and the Army general commanding these forces failed to work together. Many of the Chasseurs deserted, being mostly renegades from Napoleon's armies. The Marines, nevertheless, lived up to Commodore Popham's opinion of them, paraphrased as 'when ever the enemy came in contact with you, the result was as flattering to Britain and as honourable to the Corps, as in any similar context or battle' during the Peninsula War.

The Regiments, reorganised at different times and joined by the 3rd Marines and a

Provisional Battalion of Fleet Marines, took part in the actions summarised in Note 1 of Chapter 2 which included those on the Great Lakes and the capture of Washington. Here, by order of the British government, public buildings were burnt in reprisal for damage done to Canadian towns. They were also joined by companies of Colonial Marines, former negro slaves and probably more reliable than Gooch's Marines of 75 years before.

The Republican administration, short of money and popular support, signed a peace treaty in December 1814. News of this did not come from Europe until too late to stop the battle of New Orleans, where Gen Jackson defeated British attempts to capture this southern city. As Commander-in-Chief, the General had defeated war parties of the Cree and Choctaw Indians the previous summer. That August (1814) the British sent Maj Edward Nicolls RM to the Gulf of Mexico with a few picked men: three officers, a sergeant with local rank of lieutenant as adjutant and 108 NCOs and men. Edward Nicolls was a man of strong character, aptly called 'Fighting' Nicolls, who had been in 107 actions, wounded six times and twice court-martialled. Typical of his forceful tactics was the campaign he fought in this late summer of 1814, his small force providing the advisers and military experts in explosives who complemented the Indians' fighting techniques. To the quick raid and deadly ambush, the British added a destructive punch.

Edward Nicolls landed at Pensacola (modern Alabama), which was at that time a Spanish port in West Florida. He issued a proclamation telling the people he was head of the advance guard of a British force coming to help the Indians but they, having just been defeated by Gen Jackson, did not reform their war parties. Nevertheless 180 Indians with some local chiefs among them embarked with the Major and 72 of his men in two corvettes and two gun-brigs. These took them westward to Mobile Bay, the estuary of the Alabama River. Fifty kilometres up this river was an American fort protecting Mobile, with sea approaches through off-shore reefs. A long passage up the broad estuary took three days to negotiate, the many intricate channels first being buoyed by small boats ahead of the ships.

On the afternoon of 15 September 1814 they moored opposite this Fort Boyer, beginning the bombardment which was to prove one-sided, because the Fort's heavier guns, including 32-pounders, cut the cable of the corvette *Hermes* and she was swept onto a shoal by the strong current. The Major had landed his party, but a severe bout of dysentery had forced him to rejoin *Hermes* from where he was directing the operation. There was now no way of salvaging the corvette and she was set on fire, her crew and the Major joining the other three ships as they hauled out of range. Ashore the RMA gunners with two $5\frac{1}{2}$-in (140-mm) howitzers, found their shells made little impression on the Fort's log ramparts with their covering of earth and sods. Nor could the raiders get within 80m of the walls, for the land had been cleared around the fort. Its garrison of 300 with their 25 guns were too tough a nut to crack; the party ashore therefore marched back some 75km to Pensacola.

There the Marines began distributing the arms their rear party had been guarding. They repaired an old Spanish fort near the town and prepared for the Americans to react. This the Americans did by sending 2,000 men into West Florida to punish the Spanish for allowing British forces to use this port. Nicholls, attacked by elements of this expedition, extricated his men after killing 15 Americans and 'wounding many more'. While the autumn turned to winter in the second week in October he marched his men 400km eastward to the Apalachicola River. By this time there were some 700 Indians and Marines in the force, organised in raiding parties and a garrison for the fort they built as a firm base. This had ready access to the sea and was probably

On 17 October 1812 in the West Indies there was a fierce exchange of broadsides at close quarters between HMS *Frolic* of 18 guns and the American warship USS *Wasp* of 20 guns. *Frolic* put her jibboom over *Wasp* but, as most of the British seamen and Marines were dead or wounded, it was the *Frolic* which was boarded and captured by American sailors and Marines. Peabody Museum, Salem, Massachussetts.

not found by the Americans of Gen Macintosh, sent to contain the Indian raids.

Gen Jackson held 5,000 men in Mobile as this was a likely invasion point for any attack on New Orleans, and for a time the British had planned to land there. There were also American forces garrisoning forts on the Alabama and Cosa rivers, all of which had to be supplied from Georgia. These supply trains became a ready target for the raiders, who struck up to 120km northward to the borders of Georgia. Nicolls went briefly to join the British army approaching New Orleans and some 200km up the Mississippi, but the Commander-in-Chief would not allow him to take an active part for 'who could find another officer acquainted with Indians?'. Edward Nicolls returned to his Indian force apparently for the successful attack on Fort Boyer in mid-February 1815.

The three Marine battalions had been brigaded by this date. They came down the coast to Cumberland Island, 75km north of what in 1981 is Jacksonville Beach, Florida. Three days after they

landed, they crossed the sound to St Mary's in which they destroyed stores and defences on 12–13 January. They made other smaller raids, as the island became the fleet's principal advance base on the southern east coast until 10 March when news of the peace reached the Brigade.

These brief examples show tactics and techniques which are the origin of some commando methods in the 1980s, but they cannot show the breadth of the Marine involvement in the 18th and early 19th centuries. In those years the Corps was in action around the 'great Globe itself', the centre of their crest and cap badge, with landings as far north as the Finnish coast, south to Cape Town, Buenos Aires, Argentina, the pirate islands of the Spanish Main, eastward to the Dardanelles, Turkey, and further east in India, the Dutch East Indies and beyond. While throughout the war years Marines served in the blockading squadrons. In these decades more than any others, they earned their reputation 'for good, honest, modest service and character'.

Chapter 4

Actions around the Globe: The 19th Century

For nearly 40 years after 1815, the British were only involved in minor wars. Yet Royal Marines saw action in many of these and in the continuing war against piracy and slavers.[1] In 1816, RM detachments were with the fleet bombarding the corsair pirate stronghold of Algiers. A bold plan was made to land 'four steady men from each division' lightly armed, as covering force for Royal Engineers with storming poles. These would have been used to put explosives against casements but the problems of ship-to-shore communications were too complex and the landing was abandoned. Marine casualties from shore battery fire at the bombarding ships, were 25 killed and 125 wounded.

In 1824, as a typical year, a Royal Marine Battalion went to Bermuda, another landed in Lisbon as part of the British force of 5,000 men who were sent to help restore order after a civil war. On the Gold Coast an RMA officer planned and led the successful defence of Cape Castle, when its garrison – ravaged by fever – were attacked by 'black hordes of Ashanti'. These attacks were broken up by fire from the Marines' rocket battery and the castle's guns, before the garrison made a sally which drove the Ashanti back into the jungle. A continent away in that same year the Royal Marines of the 50-gun sailing ship HMS *Liffey* were landed in Burma with an expeditionary force from India to restore order in Rangoon. The naval squadron included the small paddle-steamer *Diana*. While *Liffey* was much like any 50-gun ship of the previous century, *Diana*'s successors in the next 30 years would change the nature of naval warfare.

Of the many actions against slavers, one in 1829 is outstanding. The 48-gun *Aibylle* with her detachment of 40 Marines was cruising off the west coast of Africa. In the many creeks and estuaries of the coast, slavers could escape the '48', but her cutter *Black Joke* had a remarkable record in capturing 21 slavers – ships often two or three times her size. Among them was the Spanish *Almirate*, a 14-gun brig with a crew of 80. She had ghosted in light airs away from *Black Joke*, but 'after an eleven hour chase with sweeps' a long pull on heavy oars, the cutter came up with her quarry.

The British crew must have backed on their oars and then pulled hard, despite their tiredness, to avoid shot from *Almirate*, while well-aimed fire from their 18-pounder took its toll, until the cutter came up on the Spaniards' quarter to force a boarding with cutlasses and bayonets. The Spanish yielded to *Black Joke*'s persistence for she had three men killed but the Spaniards had 29 casualties including 15 killed. Over 460 slaves were freed to add to the cutter's final total of 7,000 men and women freed from a life of drudgery, mostly rescued from privateers and gun-brigs.

Another action against slavers, to get ahead of the chronology of our story, took place in May 1887 when the pinnace from *Turquoise* was chasing a large dhow which turned back to attack the young officer and his four men in the small boat, but the seamen and a Marine drove them off. A single shot killed the dhow helmsman and the ship ran aground, enabling the pinnace's crew to release 53 slaves. One seaman had been killed and the other four men of this boat's crew were wounded before the 30 or more Arabs quit the dhow.

In more routine operations (if anything Royal Marines do, can be called 'routine') Fleet Marines were landed in Syria to help the Turks defeat an Egyptian army between September 1840 and 1842. 1,500 Fleet Marines, some Austrians and 5,000 Turks were landed to seize a beachhead on 10 September 1840. The escorting fleet had first sailed to the south of Beirut, drawing the Egyptian army from the town's defences, before the steamships carrying the landing force made a sudden change of course. They steamed to the beaches north of the town, before the enemy could move back to face them and the force was landed unopposed. Later that month 100 Marines were repulsed by Albanian mercenaries in a well-sited coast fort, but the Albanians withdrew and contact was made with Lebanese hill tribes, who the British then armed. There were other landings and bombardments, and a Marine garrison was landed at Acre where they lost 60 men through fever before they were withdrawn in June 1841.

Although the majority of the Corps' service continued to be at sea, Fleet Marines were frequently landed, as they were in China during the First Opium War of 1839–42. They had landed in several small actions to take enemy coast batteries after the fleet had bombarded them, before 500 Marines formed a battalion in January 1841 for the assault on Canton. They were commanded by Brevet-Maj S. B. Ellis RM 'a meritorious old officer' in his 50s, who had served at Trafalgar and in America. His battalion's skirmishers fought their way into the first complex of forts in the city's outer defences, despite being outnumbered by the Chinese. In this action one Marine went up to an enemy embrasure and fired at the gun's crew behind it, before he calmly stepped back to reload. The granite walls of these forts had seemed impregnable to bombardment, and some were double-tiered with up to 60 guns, but determined

assaults by Marines cleared many such batteries. The British had relatively modern weapons which the Chinese could not match with swords and spears, although they often fought bravely. Their Admiral Kwan, for instance, was killed by a Marine's bayonet thrust as the Admiral led the defence of Canton's north gate. It was a case of 'long knives into you or your bayonet into Johnnie Chinaman'.

Later that year, in October, Marines were again in the van of the attack when

British forces stormed Ching-hae. One of the city's magazines blew-up during the attack and in the ensuing confusion four Marines reached the city's walls but had no scaling ladder. Nevertheless they climbed some 8m up to an embrasure and forced their way into this gun position. Maj Ellis was hauled up by a rope to join them, and followed by other Marines they began clearing the ramparts. Further along the wall Vice-Admiral Sir William Parker had led a party of bluejackets up

scaling ladders and the ramparts were cleared by them and the Marines. There would be other actions in this war in which Marines sometimes landed to seize coast batteries, or stormed city ramparts under covering fire from the fleet. At other times they served in Army forces and the records show how efficiently the detachments carried out their varied roles before the Chinese sued for peace.

The last RM Artillery detachment to return to England from this war did not

The explosion of the Egyptian magazine during the bombardment of Acre on 3–4 November 1840; 1,200 people were killed and the Egyptians were forced to leave the city. In action were some of the first Royal Naval paddle-steamers, their 8-inch (20cm) guns manned by RM Artillery gunners. Engraving after Lieutenant J. F. Warre.

reach Chatham until 1847. They had spent four years in steam-sloops and frigates during actions against pirates in Brunei and elsewhere in Borneo. Their actions (they had crossed over 100km of swamp with 150 fleet Marines in one Borneo expedition) are typical of the hundreds which were fought against slavers and pirates in the last half of the 19th century. Marines during these decades also fought in Nicaragua, Malaya, Algiers, Burma, West Africa and again in China.[1]

The only major war of this period was largely fought in the Crimea (1853–56), with actions in the Baltic during the summers of 1854 and 1855. The British fleets were poorly manned, however, largely because the public's understandable resentment prevented men being pressganged. Marines once again helped to fit out ships with the *St Jean D'Acre*'s detachment of 180 Marines, a few seamen gunners and boys preparing her for sea. The expeditions to the Baltic failed to achieve any major victories, but Marines and seamen landed to attack coastal installations and the fleets bombarded coastal forts. During one of these attacks, three British ships chased a Russian war-steamer into Vyborg anchorage at the north-east head of the Gulf of Finland. On 13 July *Ruby*, with the boats of the other ships, moved towards the harbour to attack this ship, another steamer and three gunboats. The leading cutter suddenly jarred on an underwater obstruction. While the crew were trying to discover what this was, heavy fire was opened on them from a 'masked' battery some 300m away, and from the steamers. But after freeing the cutter, the boats rowed on towards the battery, trying for an hour to fight their way ashore. A spark set off a rocket in *Arrogant*'s second cutter and it went through the boat's side. The midshipman in charge was killed and the half-swamped boat drifted closer towards the battery. Petty Officer (PO) George Ingoueville, although wounded, went over the cutter's side, and grabbed the painter as he waded to prevent her from drifting closer to the beach.

Meanwhile Lt George Dare Dowell RMA, aboard *Ruby* supervising the loading of a fresh supply of rockets into his boat, saw the explosion. He called for volunteers as he jumped down into *Ruby*'s gig tied to her stern. Lt Henry Haggard RN and two seamen joined him, and they pulled for the cutter. By now the Russians had its range and grapeshot as well as musket balls whipped over the water. Nevertheless George Dowell, rowing the stroke oar, brought the gig alongside the cutter to pull three men from the water. They were rowed back to the *Ruby* and Dowell then returned to tow clear the waterlogged boat but two men had been lost and ten wounded. For their bravery in saving greater loss, PO George Ingoueville and Lt Dowell were both awarded the Victoria Cross.

In August 1854 15 British mortar vessels, each with a 13-in (330-mm) mortar manned by eight RMA gunners from the fleet, were in the bombardment of Swedborg batteries near Helsinki. These craft could carry a large supply of ammunition below decks, because the mortars were on Robert's mountings.[2] RMA officers with the fleet had planned the firing programme and on the night of 6 August the vessels were moored beyond the range of Russian guns. Next morning, at 7.15 am, they hauled themselves up to kedge anchors closing the range. For over 12 hours at a rate of 30 bombs an hour, they then plastered the granite forts of the enemy batteries. The mortars' plummeting fire caused many fires and two magazines to explode, even at its extreme range of 3,500m, before the lead-grey mortar vessels hauled off to re-ammunition. During the night artificers from the factory vessel *Volcano* repaired the cracks in mortars barrels, using molten zinc.

Near morning the vessels fired again, several being 400m closer to the shore, but by noon the mortars were so worn they were dangerous to fire. Enemy batteries had also ranged on some vessels before they were withdrawn that night, after

they had fired over 1,000 tons of bombs during the two days.

The main British campaign was fought in the Crimea. There Royal Marines fortified the hills above Balaclava, mounted guns and by early October 1854 had batteries spaced along this 1½km front known as Marine Heights. The gun crews, over 1,200 men, came from RM detachments in sailing ships, for 'those in steam-vessels, constantly under fire' could not be spared. (Although sailing ships were still part of the Black Sea Fleet in the 1850s, in the Baltic all the British ships were steam-driven or had auxillary power from steam-driven propellors.) The weather was bitterly cold but Wednesday 25 October dawned a fine if misty morning. The Marines could hear firing and as the sun cleared the early mists, a dense swarm of Russian skirmishers could be

seen driving the Turks – Britain's ally in this war – from redoubts forward of Marine Heights and to the north across a broad valley. The Marines had orders not to fire their heavy guns the 1.4km across the valley 'so as not to reveal their range'; but as the Turks fell back, the RM batteries engaged small groups of Cossacks riding down Turkish stragglers. Meanwhile the yellowish-grey coats of 3,000 Russian cavalry, with 25,000 foot soldiers and 78 guns could be seen beyond the range of the Marine Heights' batteries.

One squadron wheeled south, crossed the valley diagonally and broke over 'the thin red streak, topped with steel' of Argyll and Sutherland Highlanders to the Marines' left. Well-aimed shots from the nearest batteries 'made most excellent practice on these cavalry' in the words of the Argylls' commanding officer. The

A very early war photograph showing the British camp at Balaclava during the Crimean War. In the distance are supply ships in the narrow harbour; the Marine Heights lay beyond the hills in the background and were held by Marines from the sailing ships who mounted batteries of 12- to 32-pounder guns and some 8-inch (20cm) howitzers. The camp in the foreground housed Army troops on the Marines' left flank.

Russians retired, but 25 minutes later 2,000 of them came across the Marines' front, some within 200m of the Marines which was too close for effective shelling and too far off for the Marines' smooth-bore muskets to be sure of killing a cavalry-man. The British Heavy Brigade, 800 horsemen meticulously drawn up by their General James Scarlett, were poised at the west end of the valley. The nearest Marine batteries ceased firing and the Heavy Brigade charged. There was a flurry of hooves and flashes of sabre blades before the Brigade 'seemed swallowed up in a mass of cavalrymen'. These had halted with a second squadron 200m behind the first, and accurate fire from the Marine batteries put them in confusion. They turned back eastward along the valley, and their retreat became a rout.

Marines, reinforced by a further 600 men continued to hold the heights with such determination that the Russians mounted no major attack on them. There were, however, several skirmishes as the gunners, fighting as infantry, defended the batteries. In January 1855, light infantry training was deemed the most appropriate for Marine infantry compan-ies and they became the RM Light Infantry (RMLI). Nevertheless the Marines of infantry companies from time to time manned guns ashore, as they did afloat.

Men of the RMA joined Royal Artillery-men in setting up heavy guns to bombard Sebastopol. Gunner Fred Smith RMA was at this work when a Russian sniper began killing artillerymen. The Marine made a 600m crawl 'dragging his musket behind him' to stalk the sniper and kill him at 50 paces. Although he was in sight of the Redan – one of six stone redoubts in the walls – he crawled back undetected to his own lines.

In November 300 Marines were trans-ferred from Marine Heights to join the Light Brigade outside Sebastopol. There on the foggy morning of 5 November, after a night of heavy rain, Marines of one picket had just been relieved from their outpost. They were 'making a crude breakfast' of porridge when they heard muskets firing from the direction of the city. They could see nothing in the gloom and rain. A bugler sounded 'Fall-in'. The roll of musketry grew louder, reverberat-ing across a ravine below their hillside positions on Victoria Ridge. The Marines

A drawing showing Corporal Prettyjohns seizing the leader of a Russian patrol while other Marines hurl rocks to drive off their attackers. Prettyjohns won the Victoria Cross for this act.

advanced cautiously back towards the edge of the slope and their picket line. 'Bullets fell amongst us . . . the sergeant major was the first man killed . . . "lay down" was ordered . . . a rush of bullets passed over us . . . we gave them three rounds, [while] kneeling, into their close columns . . . seamen opened fire with some heavy guns into their left flank . . . then it was "advance" . . . [next] "hold your ground" . . .'. The four small RM companies – or those of them that could be assembled in the fog and smoke – had advanced down the line of a track off Victoria Ridge, joining the pickets on the forward slopes.

The fighting was breaking up into isolated encounters, bitterly contested, for this was *the* 'soldiers' battle' of Inkerman. These Marines' Minié rifles[3] gave no trouble but some Light Regiments had water seep from the heavy night rain into stacked weapons. As the weather began to clear, other units were also being sent forward 'to feed the pickets', which broke up the Russian columns with rifle fire. On Home Ridge the 2nd Division fought desperately to hold back the hordes, repeatedly driving them off with rifle butts and bayonets. But the grey-coated Russians at last forced these British line regiments from forward positions.

The rain had eased, the mists completely lifted about 9 am when Russian riflemen in the caves across the ravine, began picking off British officers. The Marines were ordered to clear them out; Russian guns brought up in the dark onto Inkerman Ridge, above the caves, had also begun to range on the 2nd Division atop Home Ridge.

The Russians had careened a frigate in Sebastopol harbour so that her fire lifted clear of the city walls. This shot now plummetted into the Ravine for a 'broadside thinned our ranks' and Capt William H. March RMLI was wounded. Capt Hopkins, commanding these Marines, stood 'as calm as if he was on parade . . . his cloak riddled like a sieve' by enemy shot. He sent Sgt Richards, Cpl Prettyjohns and six men to clear the caves. This they did but their ammunition was running low when a file of Russians returned to the caves. The corporal had told the men to pile boulders near the entrance, before the first Russians approached the cave mouth. Prettyjohns grabbed their

leader in a West Country wrestling grip, hurling the Russian off his feet. As he fell the Marines flung their heavy stones on the heads of the others, who tumbled off the path down the steep slope. A volley or two from the Marines' few remaining rounds, ensured this party of Russians did not return. Prettyjohns received the VC.

The following June (1855) when the siege was nearing a stalemate Bombardier T. Wilkinson RMA was in a forward trench. Russian counter-bombardment blasted his gun's position to 'all of a heap' but he climbed atop the earth-works, calling for sandbags. Despite the continuing bombardment, he began repairing the gun emplacement and others joined him, an action for which he was awarded the VC. Marines also served in the mortar vessels which in half a gale and a heavy swell on 8 September sustained a steady rate of accurate fire for three hours. The previous day a British assault on the walls had been repulsed but on the night of 9 September the Russians abandoned the city. Fleet Marines were landed near batteries at the mouth of the Dneiper in the sea of Azov. Others were landed on the Kamchatke peninsular (North Pacific) where a RM officer leading a charge against Russian positions was killed; and nearly a third of this force of 700 Fleet Marines, seamen and French Marines were casualties.

These actions in trench warfare, in mortar vessels and fitting-out ships, may at first glance seem remote not only in time but in technique from the work of Commandos in the 1980s. Yet the Royal Marines of the 19th century had a variety of jobs, just as their successors do today. Crews of the Assault Squadrons' landing craft in 1981 will recognise the difficulties in kedging a mortar vessel inshore, Malan crews can see the problems facing a rocket launch's crew trying to get a clear line of fire. These are but two parallels among several between actions of the 19th and 20th centuries. Another is the raiding practices: Fleet Marines before landing at Balaclava, for instance, had stormed the

Royal Marine Artillery batteries in action at Hernani, on 16 March 1837, covering the withdrawal of their ally the Queen of Spain's forces in the Carlist War. This might have become a rout but for their steadiness and that of the RMLI Battalion. Marines fought in Spain from May 1836 to September 1840. Painting by an unknown artist, CGRM.

Royal Marine Commando

Right: The north-east gate of Canton photographed in 1858. A few months earlier in December 1857 Marines had scaled the walls during the city's capture in the 2nd Opium War by a force of British troops.

Below: HM Gunboat *Haughty* with seamen and Marine landing parties in ships' boats, attack the shore batteries and a fleet of armed junks in Fatshan Creek, near Canton, on 1 June 1857. The assault parties landed, captured the shore batteries and despite the narrow waters captured over 70 junks which each had ten or more guns. Drawing, National Maritime Museum, London.

Danube estuary forts on 8 July 1854.

Within six months of the Peace of Paris (30 March 1856) Royal Marines were in action protecting the British 'factory' of warehouses in Canton. By the following year about 3,100 would be serving in China[1] including two Bns each of 701 Marines with 100 RMA, later joined by a Provisional Battalion of which the Sergeant Major was C/Sgt Prettyjohns VC. This Provisional Battalion originally of 570 Fleet Marines had served with the Naval Brigade during the Indian mutiny, and the 350 still serving were drafted to China.

A Brigade of 2,200 Marines was in November 1857 assembled on Wang Tang island, as part of a British force which also included 1,500 seamen in a Naval Brigade. From here they attacked the walls of Canton, principle city of southern China, and scene of actions in the opening phases of the 2nd Opium War. Despite the barbed-head Chinese rockets, stink pots and cannon fire the Marines scaled the walls on 29 December with few casualties, but Col Thomas Holloway RMA commanding the Brigade was wounded as were 18 of his men. This and other British successes made no impression on the Chinese government in Peking, and therefore the Taku forts were occupied. These defences at the entrance to the Pei-ho river blocked access to its river port of Tientsin and the capital, Peking, further inland.

With the forts in British hands, however, the Chinese signed the peace of Tientsin in May 1858, and the Taku forts were handed back to the Chinese. This treaty was broken in the following June by the refusal among other things to allow British and French Ministers to reach Peking – the 3rd Opium War began.

British and French squadrons escorting their Ministers found that the Taku forts had been repaired, and three booms or barriers blocked the river. Matting over the embrasures made it difficult to know how many guns had been mounted, but some could be seen from the British ships which were nine steam gunboats and a sloop. The deep-drafted unarmed French ships lay off the estuary, when early in the afternoon of 25 June 1859 Rear-Admiral James Hope sent *Opossum* to pull out iron piles in the seaward barrier. Her crew worked one loose and had started on the second when at 2.40 pm the forts opened fire. In the next four hours the gunboats took heavy punishment as they tried to force their way past the barriers. Early in the action an American double-banked cutter (two men to each oar) rowed past the first barrier. She carried Flag Officer Josiah Tatnall USN who had fought the British in 1812, his ships as neutrals lay off the estuary while he boarded *Plover* to talk to Admiral Hope, who had been wounded. The American seamen, showing more fight than their neutrality strictly allowed, helped man *Plover*'s forward gun and several were wounded before the cutter withdrew.

About 7 pm the forts had virtually ceased firing and Admiral Hope decided to land Fleet Marines to capture them. The American flagship towed in their boats from ships in the bay, as she came into the river to take out wounded. Capt Charles Shadwell RN took command of the 350 Marines, Royal Engineers with scaling ladders, 60 French sailors and a few bluejackets. Lt-Col Thomas Lemon RMA, who had commanded the 1st Marines in China for seven months, advised against the attack but the Admiral sent the boats in at 7.20 that evening. Almost immediately they came under fire from the fort on the north bank as they struggled across 500m of muddy foreshore towards the south bank. There three forts with probably 1,500 gunners, were also ready. The Marines found three deep ditches on the marshy banks, with sharpened bamboo stakes beneath their slime. They struggled and heaved themselves through the sludge, 50 reaching an outer bastion's ramparts, where several were killed by Tartar bowmen's arrows. The only scaling ladder was pushed up against this wall but three men were killed and

Royal Marine gun crews in a 32-pounder battery above the 'Left Attack' positions before Sebastopol in 1855. Seamen can be seen hauling up another 32-pounder and forward picket lines can be seen in the left centre of the picture. Painting by an unknown artist, CGRM.

five wounded as they climbed it. With cartridges soaked and too few ashore to storm the walls, a withdrawal was ordered. With calm deliberation as it grew dark, wounded were first sent back, then in organised sections men made their way to the boats – the tide flooding which shortened the distance they had to press their tired legs through the mud.

Lt H. L. Evans RMLI, the Adjutant, had been up to the ramparts and made three trips to the boats with wounded men. The night, bright with Chinese fireballs and rockets, gave little cover and the Chinese continued to fire as the Marines retreated. Evans, nevertheless, was one of the last to leave when the evacuation was completed at 1.30 am (26 June).

In this unfortunate affair 15 men had been killed, 252 wounded and 15 drowned in the slime, more than the total British casualties at the famous battle of Cape St Vincent (1797). When the allies returned to the area in August 1860, they avoided the forts, putting 18,000 men ashore north of the Pei-ho. This force included an RMLI Battalion and RMA gunners; it reached Peking in October before a peace treaty was signed. Marines would continue to serve ashore and in ships of the China station over the years – and were serving in Hong Kong in 1981. (For changes in Corps strength over these years see Note 4.)

The British did not conscript men, once the pressgangs ceased to practice in the 1850s, although the legal power to do so remained until 1871. Prussia, however, had done so since the 18th century and only in 1814 limited this service to five years. France reintroduced it in 1818. But the first RM conscripts did not join until

Above: The Royal Marines' camp on the San Juan Islands *c.* 1860. These Marines and a detachment of the US Marine Corps jointly garrisoned the islands from July 1859 until their ownership passed to the United States. The RM detachment was then withdrawn in November 1872.

Left: British troops in camp at the Taku Forts after their capture from the Chinese in June 1900.

Above: 18 British, French, Dutch and American ships bombard the batteries of the Japanese Prince Choshiu at Shimonoseki on 4 October 1864. The prince opposed foreigners trading in Japan and resisted the landing of an RM battalion with detachments from the ships. The Marine battalion lost 1 killed and 12 wounded in driving off the enemy.

Right: Royal Marines with US Marines manning a Maxim gun at the 'Fort Halliday' strong point in the defence of the British Legation in Peking, 1900.

Below: Royal Marines and troops with a field gun in Tsientsin during operations to relieve the legation in Peking in mid-1900.

after the passing of the National Service Act of 1916. Before then there was a strong British tradition for voluntary service, originally in the home defence militia and by 1899 in the yeomanry. This home defence force of mounted infantry attracted many volunteers when the Boer War (1899–1902) broke out in southern Africa. The British enthusiasm stemmed from the hostility of much of Europe, a threat which obliged the Admiralty to keep Marines in the fleet. For since 1885 all Marines had been able to gain the same specialist qualification (SQ) ratings in gunnery as seamen and the RMLI, as much as the RMA, manned big ships' guns.

Boer forces entered British Natal on 12 October 1899, believing that a quick victory might bring one or two European countries – Germany and the Netherlands – to their aid. The Boers expected quickly to isolate the small British garrisons in major towns, for the Boers fought in highly mobile Commando columns of 400

Companies of the RMLI after storming the lines at Tel-el-Kebir on 13 September 1882. They had advanced over 800m 'at the double' to storm the Egyptian trenches.

For nearly 50 years the Taku Forts at the entrance to the Pei-ho river were a key defence in Chinese strategy, but in 1900 an Allied force captured the forts and their guns were dismantled by detachments of Royal Marines.

A halt in the Bayuda desert during the Royal Marine Camel Company's operations in Egypt from January to May 1885. The company of 97 all ranks served in the Guards Camel Regiment. Painting by Bartelli, 45 Commando RM.

Right: In 1884 Marines fought in a number of actions against the Sudanese while garrisoning the Red Sea port of Suakin with forts (Fort Hasheen is shown). The Marine battalion was withdrawn in April 1885 but a mounted company stayed to carry out raids until June.

Below: A ceremonial occasion of the 1890s. New colours were presented to the Royal Marines at Chatham on 22 June 1896 by the Duke of Saxe-Coburg and Gotha (Duke of Edinburgh) (centre front). Among those present were Colonel Commandant Colwell, CB.

Opposite above: Royal Marine battalions served with the Army in Egypt 1886 and are shown landing at Ismailia.

Opposite below: An officer making his night rounds of the troop-deck aboard HMS *Orontes* in the 1880s.

or so, which could cover distances far greater than British or Indian infantry, without need of supply columns, as a small bag of rusks, a pocketful of *biltong* (sun dried beef) and a little coffee could last a Boer horseman for a week.

He also had a fighting tradition, like his namesake the commando of the 1980s, which went back to the mid-19th century. Then, living in isolated farms the Boer had to be supremely self-reliant to survive in hostile territory. He fought without any of the sentiment of European soldiery, wishing to get to close quarters with his enemy. For the Boer his musket and later his rifle was his means of killing an enemy be it lion or man. He was, therefore, dependent on his skill as a good shot, his pony trained to stand steady until the last moment to withdraw. These men formed the Commandos – originally as hunting parties – to clear a valley of hostile tribes or wild life. Their officers did not have

executive authority but led by example as any officer must in fighting that does not have the shape of a set-piece battle.

Military training was limited to the rifle practice encouraged in the Boer Republics, but every man's daily life on the broad veldt grassland gave him the keen eyesight, the horsemanship and experience of frugal living which made him a first-class soldier. His tactics would give war a mobility not seen for several centuries – not since the Mongul hordes had swept into Europe – for only 500 Boers were needed to cover a kilometre of front 'line'. Yet Wellington had needed 12,000 men per kilometre at Waterloo in 1815 and in the very different conditions of Mukden (1905) the Russians had 5,000 per kilometre. Rapid-firing small arms were also to make their first impact in this war, the Boers' Mausers having a magazine with five rounds and the British Lee-Metford's eight rounds. The machine gun's forerunners had been in use for some years – Marines in the Sudan were in action in 1884 with naval Gardener guns – but their

complexity made the War Office reluctant to adopt the machine gun until World War I.

After the Boers had advanced into Natal, troops from India were landed to help relieve its British garrisons, and Fleet Marines were landed with seamen, initially to garrison Durban. The seamen had two 12-pounders on mountings improvised by Capt Percy Scott RN, who also designed mobile mountings for naval 4.7-in (119-mm) guns. The latter's range – an RMA crew knocked out a Boer 6-in gun at 10km – proved effective, but the armour-piercing shells they sometimes used had their drawbacks in a land battle. The Marines were reorganised in November to form a small battalion of 190 Marines and 50 seamen with two 12-pounders, which joined Lord Methuen's column marching to the relief of Kimberley. His force of two infantry brigades, 850 cavalry and mounted infantry, four companies of Royal Engineers and two RA field batteries, was formidable enough on paper to break through the loose forma-

Right : Royal Marine gunners in 1897 training on the 12-pounder field gun, which had a range of 1,800m. The School of Land Artillery at Fort Cumberland near Eastney (where these men were training) continued until the 1940s.

Opposite above : A Boer Commando – from which the name 'Commando' originates – in positions overlooking the main Mafeking–Krugersdorp road. This Commando is flying the Vierkleur flag of their republic.

Opposite below : An armoured train of the Boer War. This one is carrying Royal Marines and seamen who could have fired through slits in the trucks' armoured sides if necessary.

tions of Boer Commandos easily, yet on 24 November the Boers successfully held up the column's advance.

At 3 am that morning a night attack by the Guards and 9th Brigades failed to dislodge an estimated 6,000 Boers. The naval 12-pounders were then brought forward from the armoured train advancing with the column. Their greater range than that of the field guns was used to good effect in searching the flat hill tops of the Boers' positions. The guns had opened fire at 3,000m causing their mules to bolt and Marines then hauled the guns forward

'following the galloping field gunners' to about 1,500m from the Boers' low hills, where the guns again fired at about 8.30 am. Enemy fire was slight and the only two Marine casualties were caused by sunstroke. Early next day (25 November) cavalry patrols at 5.45 am found the Boers had withdrawn to a second line of low hills, the Graspan. Here covering a 5km front, their flanks were drawn back to protect the line, with a clear field of fire for 3km for the grass was only 45cm high and the only other cover was an occasional ant hill.

In two hours British guns silenced the positions on the Marines' left, before they, 50 bluejackets and a company of the Kings Own Yorkshire Light Infantry (KOYLI) were ordered 'to advance inclined to the right'. A difficult manoeuvre on a level parade ground, but almost impossible through grass with each man marching diagonally to his right front while trying to keep abreast of the others. When they were 700m from the hills, the artillery fire stopped; but had to begin shelling again, for in the next 100m heavy and accurate fire came from the left,

enfilading the Marines' advancing line. Each man had begun by instinct rather than orders, to march straight to his front but as they came forward men began to fall. They were 'ordered to lie prone' and fire volleys, but with the men spread along the line these were difficult to control. Then they were up, advancing in short rushes 'like clockwork, without hesitation'. The second or third rush brought them 300m from the rock face of the hills, an ideal range for Mausers and many were hit. The men, most of them under fire for the first time, calmly adjusted their rifle sights at each pause of the advance.

About 100m from the crags, the Boers' fire began to slacken. Then the Marines were up and dashing to the foot of the rocks, where they paused to catch their breath, for here they were out of sight of the Boers above them. The Marines scrambled halfway up the face, paused to form a line and went on up to within 25m of the crest before the last Boers retired. Over the crest, the line again came under fire from the left and a second ridge of hills, but in the distance Boer waggons

Privates of the RM Light Infantry in their barrack room at Forton Barracks in 1900.

could be seen trekking north 'as hard as they could go'. The price of victory had been eight killed, including Capt Guy Senior RMA killed in the second rush and Maj John H. Plumb killed as he led the dash for the base of the crags. And there were 83 Marines wounded from the 180 who had made the attack. The KOYLI and the bluejackets also had heavy casualties. Cdr A. P. Ethelston RN was killed and Capt Alfred E. Marchant RMLI appointed in his place, the first RM officer for many years to command a naval brigade which included seamen.

The use of Marines and seamen as assault infantry was criticised at that time, for they were 'expensive products . . . many with scientific training . . . who cannot be produced at all except after long preparation'. The Marines, therefore, returned to their ships in September 1900 and as over 10,000 yeomanry were in

South Africa – their expenses mainly paid by voluntary contributions – the War evolved into an almost entirely Army commitment.

Some RM officers were seconded to these forces, however, including signals and military intelligence specialists. The Corps signal branch had been established over a decade; and three years after the first Marconi wireless telegraphy sets were installed in ships, RM officers' duties in 1903 included: 'taking charge of W/T in those ships not carrying a torpedo officer'. Naval intelligence had been and would continue to be a field in which a number of RM officers specialised.

The Commandos would inherit more than a name from the Boer horsemen of the Veldt, but their use as line infantry is a waste of their talents, even if at times it is unavoidable. As in World War I, when use of Marines in trench warfare was a

The Sea Service Battery for training RMA gunners at Eastney still possessed some muzzle-loaded guns until March 1898, but it was then completely equipped with breech-loading guns (as shown), and a year later some QF (Quick Firing) guns were installed.

mis-use of specialist forces, although as that war went on, there would be fewer and fewer of the highly trained gunners in proportion to the 'Hostility Only' (HO) recruits in the Corps.

Four holders of the Victoria Cross. *Above left:* Capt (later General Sir) Lewis S. Tollemache Halliday VC, RMLI: awarded the VC for leading a sortie of 20 Marines in defence of the Peking Legation during the Boxer Rising, 1900. *Above right:* Cpl (later Sergeant) John Prettyjohns VC: for gallantry at the Battle of Inkerman (see p. 61). *Below left:* Bombardier Thomas Wilkinson VC: for gallant conduct in the advanced batteries before Sebastopol, 1855 (see p. 63). *Below right:* Lt George Dare Dowell VC, RMA: for going to the aid of a rocket-boat's crew under heavy fire. All are portraits by unknown artists; RM Museum, Eastney.

Chapter 5

World War I: Trench Warfare, Battleships and Opposed Raids

When the Germans advanced into France and Belgium in August 1914 an RM Brigade[1] was formed in five days as a 'Flying Column'. They were landed at Ostend and later sent to Antwerp where they were in action for several days. Meanwhile five officers and 200 other ranks, served in Cdr Samson's Royal Naval Air Service armoured cars, in the open country north of Dunkirk. This squadron of cars harassed German cavalry patrols to such good effect that the Germans believed these 'Motor Bandits' were the advance guard of a major force.[2]

After their return from Belgium the Brigade was reorganised as the 3rd Brigade of the Royal Naval Division and sent to the Dardanelles. Each battalion with its stores was loaded onto transports ready to carry out raids against Turkish forts and cover seamen demolishing these. One such raid was made before the Brigade passed from Royal Navy to Army command and they were landed on the Gallipoli peninsula which forms the north shore of the Dardanelles Strait.

The Plymouth Battalion were landed with a company of 2nd South Wales Borderers on 'Y' beach early on the morning of 25 April without opposition. 'Y' beach was a narrow strip of sand below 60-m cliffs, which the Turks had thought too difficult a point for a landing. Two RM Companies advanced inland, found no defences and returned to join others dug-in on the cliff top. These 'trenches' were little more than scrapes and were inadequate cover when the Turks began shelling the cliff top. About 5.30 pm Turks from a battalion moved across the peninsula that afternoon, probed the Marines' positions. The first attacks were held off, but after dark the sounds of marching men could be heard with snatches of Turkish orders shouted down the wind. These were drowned from time to time in the crash of shell fire heralding another Turkish attack. Col Godfrey Matthews, CO of the Battalion, moved from company to company, reassuring the men, many of whom were young recruits of 17 and 18. Covering fire from the warships broke up a major attack just at first light but two 6-inch shells fell short and burst into one RM company's position. The Turks came storming forward, over-running several forward positions, to near the cliff top. The Colonel led his last reserves, some 40 men, who with bayonets and rifle butts drove back the Turks. This was the last Turkish attack on this beachhead but the possibility of exploiting the situation was missed, for the landing force commander's energies were absorbed in the bloodbath on 'V' and 'W' beaches. The Plymouth battalion was withdrawn, but a party of seamen looking for wounded found no Turks on 'Y' beach later that day.

Three days later the Brigade landed at Anzac beach and were repeatedly in action during the next ten months, here or on other sections of the Gallipoli front. They were the last to be withdrawn on the night of 8 January 1916, having been the first to land albeit in a raid on Turkish forts early in March 1915.

In a very different action Royal Marines with the capital ship and cruiser squadrons were in action on 31 May 1916. The opening shots of what became the Battle of Jutland were fired by the battle cruisers

Gunners of the RMA are deployed as infantry in an outpost of the Ostend, Belgium defences on 28 August 1914 in the first month of World War I.

Lützow at 3.48 pm and by the British Battle Cruiser Squadrons three minutes later. The range was 16.6km and the fire effective, for the 'Q' Turret's roof was blown off on the British ship *Lion*. Maj Francis J. W. Harvey RMLI was badly wounded but as commander of the turret gave orders to flood the magazines. This saved the battle cruiser, for a second explosion in the turret 'passed right down and through the turret in a great sheet of flame' killing all the men who had evacuated the magazine. By 4 pm the range had

A Vickers of the RM Machine Gun Sections in action at Gallipoli in 1915.

narrowed to just over 15km, and a few minutes later the battle cruiser *Indefatigable* blew up.

Four British battleships then joined the action as they came up, the main German fleet coming into action at 4.46 pm. The British 5th Battle Squadron, however, was not in range until some 80 minutes later, after which a running fight continued into the night.

One of the light cruisers present was the *Chester*, which had on board an RMLI detachment of 40 who manned two of her 5.5-in guns, half as gun crews and half with action stations in gunnery control, magazines and shell rooms. At 5.30 pm the *Chester* came into action against three German light cruisers. The Germans' fourth salvo – their shooting was of a high order that day – at 5km range, hit the *Chester*'s port side. Three guns' crews were killed or wounded and the port No. 1 gun knocked out. Capt E. Bamford RMLI, stepped from the shattered control room aft, with a minor wound. Immediately he joined the depleted crew of one gun, while controlling its fire and that of a second '5.5'. Two Marines came up from the shell room party below, to help keep the two RM guns in action. Both were killed, the guns nevertheless continued firing.

As dawn broke British destroyers put in the final attack of the action, sinking the old battleship *Pommern*. She was one of the Germans' few losses in the battle, having 11 ships sunk and 2,550 dead from their crews totalling 45,000. The British lost 14 ships – most of them larger vessels than the Germans' – with 6,090 men killed from the 60,000 men who took part. Royal Marines formed nearly 10% of the Royal Navy crews, with 5,832 in action. (The Corps losses were 538 killed.)

Maj J. W. Harvey was awarded a posthumous VC and Capt Bamford the DSO, and there were other awards to Marines. A tribute to the tenacity of Royal Marine Commandos, if not to their techniques. The German Navy undoubtedly had a victory in material terms,

having sunk 155,000 tons of British warships for the loss of only 61,000 tons, although this had no direct effect on the overall state of the war, thereafter the Germans concentrated on building up their U-boat fleets.

The main struggle by 1916 was in France and Belgium, where the rate of attrition of trench warfare was exacting a high price from a generation of Europeans. The 1st and 2nd RMLI battalions were brought to France from Gallipoli, in May and reorganised; their strength again was each brought up to 1,000 men and they were re-equipped and formed into machine gun companies. By July these battalions formed with Howe and Anson Battalions of seamen the 188th Brigade of the renamed 63rd (Royal Naval) Division.[1] They went into the line on a relatively quiet sector of the front on 14 July. The original method of holding the front and support lines in strength was no longer tenable under artillery barrages; therefore the front line and support line had become 'in effect a line of sentry groups and a line of pickets'. Although the latter were still connected by a trench, the front (first) line was a series of strong points (posts) with the support (second) line intended to delay any major attack and block local ones. The third line was generally the principal line of resistance, held by two companies (probably 400 men but on paper over 500) on a 700m battalion front. They had dug-outs, machine guns and trench mortars, the whole system giving a depth to the defence of several hundred metres where possible.

Trench warfare is a role for heavy infantry, and not suited to the style of commando tactics. Nevertheless many commandos in World War II would spend long periods (2 or 3 months) in the line,

The scrub covered cliffs of Cape Helles, the south-east point of the Gallipoli peninsular, along which RM battalions were in action from April 1915 with few breaks until RM companies covered the final withdrawal in January 1916

Royal Marines of 1900 to
1923. *Left to right:*
  1. Gunner RMA in
     working dress of 1916;
  2. Corporal RMLI in 1900
     Marching Order;
  3. Private RMLI in khaki
     Marching Order 1917;
  4. Officer RMLI in Mess
     Dress of 1900;
  5. Officer RMLI in
     Review Order of 1908;
  6. Musician RMA in 1910
     Review Order cap;
  7. Officer RMA in
     Review Order of 1900;
  8. Officer RMA in
     Undress of 1922;
  9. Officer RMA in Mess
     Dress of 1900;
 10. Drummer RMLI in
     Review Order of 1922;
 11. Officer RMLI in Drill
     Order of 1904;
 12. Field Officer RMA in
     Drill Order of 1914;
 13. Gunner RMA in the
     working dress worn in
     South Africa in 1917;
 14. Senior NCO RMLI in
     Tropical Dress of 1900.
Painting by Charles C.
Stadden, RM Museum,
Eastney.

for they could not be replaced by line infantry. That they did not let trench warfare blunt their aggressive tactics is referred to in the next chapter. The Germans in World War I developed special battalions, *Stosstrupen*, for storming exceptionally stubborn defences or complex strong points. These élite forces' methods were well known to the British Army Officers, who founded the British Commandos early in World War II. For the Royal Marines, the trench warfare of 1915–18 was to provide an experience of infantry tactics which complemented their knowledge of naval gunnery.

The 1st and 2nd RMLI (consolidated as 1st RMLI in April 1918) were to be in action along the western front at regular intervals from July 1916 until the armistice on 11 November 1918. A summary of these operations is given in Note 3, but one example shows something of the grim conditions of this trench warfare. The RMLI Battalions, 1/RMLI and 2/RMLI,

had come out of the line in the third week of July, 1917, and were training replacements. By this date the second-in-command, with some other officers and two Company Sergeant Majors, remained with the transport when the battalion made an attack, for the losses had been so great throughout the British Army that battalions had to be virtually re-formed after an attack.

On the night of 2 October, the Marines marched from training areas behind Arras to entrain for the north. Marching in World War I, when a man carried 44kg, compared to the 27kg in the 1980s, had been a tedious affair of 30km or more a day in 1916, along straight French roads lined by poplar trees, in exhausting bitter winds during the winter months. Railways, the only means of moving large land forces at that time, took the 63rd (RN) Division to training areas behind the Ypres salient, and it came under the command of XVIII Corps. They then spent over a

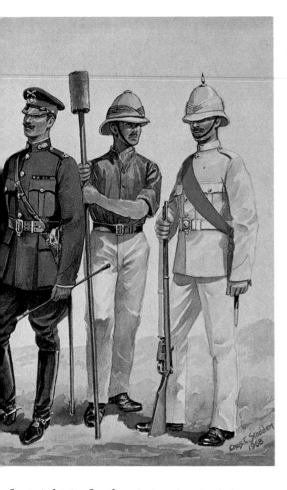

shell-holes', were in such a poor state that men would not survive in them more than 36 hours under artillery fire. This left little time for reconnaissance, not that much could be identified in this natural swamp. (Farmers had drained it but shell-fire – 4.3 tonnes on every metre of the front – had destroyed the channels and ditches that had earlier carried away the swamp water.) The German concrete redoubts could be seen, but apparently were not connected by trenches. Such defence works[4] required direct hits from heavy shells to make much impression on them, while the Germans in deep bunkers near these defences were comparatively safe. These redoubts on the 'blue' map-line of first objectives for 1/RMLI lay across 800m of otherwise featureless wastes. This was a broad front for a battalion of 600 men to attack and on their right was Anson Battalion on a 550m front, giving the Brigade a two-battalion front. On 1/RMLI's left would be a battalion of the 58th Division. Once 1/RMLI and Anson reached their 'blue' line objectives, 2/RMLI (on the left) and Howe were to pass through to attack across the Padde-beek stream, where a second series of strong points supported those of the first series.

At 8 pm on 25 October a skirmishing platoon and two sections of 1/RMLI moved forward to a white tape laid for their start line. They lay there soaked and no doubt fearful for the next 10 hours. By 2 am (26 October) all the companies were deployed (603 all ranks) and waited crouching in shell-holes waist deep in water. In moving forward they had to be careful not to miss the 'recognised' route, for a man could be swallowed up in this swamp and many were. Each platoon had been given objectives, but when the covering barrage opened at 5.40 am they were hard pressed to keep up with it. Slipping and sloshing in the half light, a Marine would find a moment's cover in a shell-hole, then stagger on. The next minute he might be knee-deep in liquid mud, before scurrying over firmer ground to keep

fortnight in further intensive training.

The three Brigades of the Division were to mount an attack on the line of enemy strong points facing a canal bank 1,000m north of Ypres. Across their front ran the muddy Paddebeek stream about 600m further north of the canal, adding to the watery quagmire of this front which had been worsened by the wet autumn weather. The farmland, riddled by shell fire, had therefore become almost impracticable for any co-ordinated attack.

Nevertheless, 189th Brigade moved into the line at Passchendaele so that the 188th could pass through to attack on 26 October, and the 190th would follow up with a second attack four days later. As the RMLI Battalions moved into the forward lines on the night of 25 October, Hood Battalion was in the support lines ready to block any counter-attack and another battalion of the 189th, Hawke Battalion, was in reserve.

The forward trenches, a mere 'line of

pace with the barrage. There was no way the leading three skirmish columns could contact each other.

It did not matter that mud and the stench of decay clung to the Marines' clothes, on puttees up to the knee and water squelched into their boots, but an SMLE rifle bolt or the mechanism of a Lewis gun (prone to jam in the best conditions) could become useless when mud choked them. Ammunition, especially in machine guns, might also jam if covered in mud. Not surprisingly, therefore, the Mills grenade and the overlong 17-in steel bayonet, were the weapons a man expected to use. With these, 1/RMLI's platoons fought their way into their objectives. As they advanced, the battalion on their left failed to keep up with the barrage, and German machine guns were able therefore to take a heavy toll of the platoons on the left. There was no question of neatly arranged company attacks following the skirmishers' small columns; it was a platoon commander's battle and they won it. Despite heavy German defensive shell fire, the Adjutant, Capt H. B. Van Praagh, led a section or so forward to reinforce a captured German strong point, just as a German counter-attack developed. When this had been repulsed, the Adjutant made a recce towards the second line of objectives, learning much he would later explain to platoons of 2/RMLI when they passed through.

Many platoon commanders by this time (about 6 o'clock) were dead or wounded. 2nd Lt W. C. Williamson, despite his wounds, led one platoon forward to bomb their way into a strong point. On the left, Sgt Priestley, taking command when his platoon officer was hit, saw Germans preparing to attack the flank. His platoon killed or captured all 50 of them.

Despite the terrible conditions 1/RMLI held the 'blue' line, having taken all their objectives; on their right Anson also held all of their objectives except one, a farmhouse – or the remains of it – on the right flank. 2/RMLI passed through the 'blue' line at 7.36 am following the barrage now

Beaumont Hamel, with the rubble of its church, in the sector of the Somme front where in November 1916 1/RMLI lost 132 killed and 210 wounded from a strength of about 500 – 2/RMLI had similar losses with only one officer surviving the attacks they put in. These made an advance of about 500m.

moving towards their objectives. In the centre, between platoons of C Company on the left and those of A on the right, resistance was strong. On the flanks, however, they made some progress. Capt J. Peter Ligertwood (a sergeant commissioned in 1916), led men of his A Company across the Paddebeek. Each of its four platoons carried a red flag, which acted as a rallying point; but to help men keep to the narrow tracks of firm ground across the swamp, they were linked by lengths of spun yarn.

Peter Ligertwood was hit three times as they moved towards five 'organised shell-holes' where German pickets with machine guns held posts between their two sets of redoubts. A Company cleared these, leaving soldiers to man them, and then advanced towards the remains of a farm and a very solid concrete blockhouse. The Captain was wounded for the fourth time and had to be carried back – he later died of these wounds – but he pointed out a route to the next objective before leaving his men. The positions were so badly defined that on the left wing of the Brigade's advance, C Company were not certain they had reached the limits set for their advance. The Battalion Adjutant, Capt Newling was killed, as was CSM W. W. Love. Lt F. C. Balcombe led a bayonet charge carrying a rifle himself, to clear another strong point but was killed a little later, because despite their efforts the 2/RMLI could not hold the ground beyond the Paddebeek.

B Company, the reserve, were committed and became absorbed into five strong posts 300 to 400m north of the old front line. The Battalion's machine gunners were brought into action, their officers making recces to ensure these guns would be well sited, and moving them to new positions when enemy fire knocked out the old. Four of these machine guns were on mobile mountings; and so skilfully brought into action – after their lieutenant had made a dangerous recce – that they had few casualties. The machine gun companies later 'maintained

HMS *Vindictive* is held alongside Zeebrugge mole by HMS *Daffodil* while Royal Marines of the 4th Battalion and seamen storm ashore up the remaining gangways under heavy German fire. Painting by de Lacey, CGRM.

a complicated barrage' which helped to break up German counter-attacks that afternoon. Shell fire was less effective since the mud absorbed much of their blast. At dusk the last outposts of A Company were driven back over the stream, and a company of seamen was sent up to support the five posts by the stream. D Company of 2/RMLI had continued throughout the battle to carry forward ammunition reserves and water.

The 1st and 2nd RMLI hung on all that night, consolidating their positions before handing over the new 'line' to Hawke Battalion at 5 am (27 October). Their achievement at the cost of 679 casualties, over half their strength, was a few hundred metres advance and the other battalions gained even less ground. The whole action, like those to follow in the next couple of weeks, were intended to absorb German reserves, but these were still available and in contrast the British had used all their reserves in trying to achieve numerical superiority. The RMLI battalions would suffer many more casualties, becoming so few in numbers, despite replacements, that at the end of April 1918 they merged to form the only RMLI battalion in France.[1] [2]

Another important reason for the lack of RM replacements for the battalions in France was the formation of the 4th RM Battalion which was to land at Zeebrugge. There a major amphibious raid was mounted to cover the sealing of the canal to Bruges with block ships and so imprison the German U-boats and torpedo-boats based at Bruges.

The raiding parties to be landed on the mole at Zeebrugge – 703 Royal Marines of the 4th Battalion and 200 seamen – were in about equal numbers to the German infantry and gun crews defending the 2.4km of this stone sea wall. At 5 pm on 22 April 1918, as the old cruiser *Vindictive* steamed north from the Thames, she received Admiral Roger Keyes' signal 'St George for England'. She and the two Mersey ferries *Iris* and *Daffodil* were to land the assault parties just after midnight,

the early morning of St George's day. Plans had been carefully laid and the ships specially equipped. All the men were ready with a remarkable cheerfulness when the battalion went to action stations at 11 pm. They carried little besides their rifles, bayonets, two grenades apiece and 60 rounds, until casualties increased the survivors' loads. Some men had weighted coshes, boy buglers had cutlasses. All of them wore steel helmets, with respirators on the chest over khaki drill under which was an inflatable life-belt.

The Battalion's Adjutant, Capt Arthur R. Chater, a veteran of Antwerp (1914) and Gallipoli although only 22, went up to join the commanding officer Lt-Col B. N. Elliot DSO on the signal bridge. Here, he also found to his surprise, was the second-in-command, who had decided to stay with the Colonel until *Vindictive* was alongside the mole.

Vindictive intended to land her force just opposite the fortified section at the seaward end of the defences. Here they would storm the gun batteries, light flares to guide three block ships and secure the defences, holding them long enough to allow these ships to enter the harbour and scuttle in the Bruges (Belgium) canal which flowed into it. Arthur Chater could hear gunfire ahead as *Vindictive* altered course for her final run towards the high outer wall of the mole. A star shell burst away to the left, then more lit the sky nearer the ship; their hard white light cast deep shadows, but he could clearly see individual faces among the Portsmouth and Plymouth companies at the foot of the ramps leading to the landing deck. (This had been built-up to match the level of the mole's outer wall.)

Enemy guns had been firing for the past quarter of an hour, but *Vindictive* was hidden in wreaths of heavy smoke that issued from floats laid down by British motor-torpedo boats. There would be no chance of surprise, nor because of mists and rain could the RAF bomb the harbour as had been planned. The German gunners, therefore, were ready and had no

Left: The long gangways slung from the improvised boat deck of HMS *Vindictive* were to be lowered onto the outer wall of Zeebrugge mole in the raid by 4th RM Battalion. However, all but two were shot away as *Vindictive* approached the mole.

Below: The Mersey ferryboat HMS *Daffodil* with her seamen demolition party and their covering guard of 22 NCOs and men of the 4th RM Battalion. Her sister ship HMS *Iris* carried 'A' (Chatham) Company of the battalion who took heavy casualties after attempts to secure her alongside the Zeebrugge mole had failed.

Barbed wire defences on the Zeebrugge mole, which were attacked by the 4th RM's survivors before they were recalled to HMS *Vindictive*.

distractions when a sudden shift in the wind cleared the smoke.

Captain A. F. B. Carpenter RN (*Vindictive*) raised his speed as soon as he saw the mole clearly 300m away on the port bow. The ship swung to 45° across the tide, a searchlight snapped on to illuminate the cruiser, and every German gun that would bear opened fire. Arthur Chater crouched under the cover of the bridge's splinter-proof 'mattresses' – he had been wounded twice in earlier actions – but his senior officers, not hearing or not heeding his advice to do the same, remained standing as they looked at the wet jade-green gentle curve of the wall. The next second a shell burst below the signal bridge and the CO and second-in-command fell dead.

The Pom-Poms in the fighting top had opened fire, the signal for all of *Vindictive*'s guns to do the same, but her surge of power had brought her 300m further down (shoreward) on the mole than intended. The noise was appalling; despite

the cotton wool stuffed in his ears to one Marine it felt as if 'the sky was falling', as he lay prone for a little cover on the deck. A German destroyer a mere 100m away inside the mole, let fly to add to the batteries' fire. Machine guns chattered persistently; German riflemen took more specific aim. 'Even then [above the great noise] we could hear the wails of anguish of the dying and wounded.' Chater reported to C Company's commander who took charge of the Battalion, but casualties were mounting, and especially so on the starboard side, without the protection built-up on the port hand which was expected to be alongside the mole.

Nos. 10 and 11 Platoons (C Company) had lost most of their men here before *Vindictive*'s bow was against the wall. The naval captain leading the seamen was killed but they managed to get two of the long gangways (brows) across to the wall. Up the one on the left went Lt-Cdr Bryan Adams RN with a party of seamen, on the right Arthur Chater led No. 5 Platoon of B Company, as the brow sawed up and down with the motion of the ship. It was at such a steep angle that you needed all your concentration to keep your balance, as one Marine later wrote: 'I forgot about the rain of lead and really felt comfortable when I put my foot on "concrete".'

From the top of the outer wall, the men dropped down a metre or so to a narrow promenade-walk with railings on the inboard side. Their rubber-soled gym shoes gave them a grip on the stonework. The seamen moved out along the walkway towards the seaward outer battery, No. 5 Platoon turned right along the wall to attack German riflemen firing into *Vindictive* from a shed roof 100m away. The OC, Lt T. F. Cooke, was wounded before he had moved far, but he continued to direct his men's fire which apparently drove the Germans from the roof.

Star shells and a searchlight's glow made the night so bright you could see men moving in the open: opportunities not missed by German machinegunners close to the landing point, but there was no time to hang about for in 20 minutes or less the blockships would be passing the end of the mole. Chater looked down from the walkway railings to see that there was a 6-metre drop to the wide roadway of the mole. Because this was too far for men to jump, he had hooked-ropes slung from the railings. No. 9 Platoon (C Company) led by Lt C. R. W. Lamplough next came up the brow and followed 'No. 5'. They and the 12 survivors of No. 10 Platoon (35 were already casualties) slid down the ropes and bombed their way into No. 3 Shed. This they made into a defended position which would prevent any German reinforcements reaching the seaward batteries. As they were doing this, Lewis gunners got into a fire fight with the small German destroyer and the Marines even tossed a few Mills grenades into her.

About the time No. 9 Platoon climbed down the ropes, Serg-Maj C. Thatcher organised scaling ladders on the wall, seamen Lewis gunners killing the half dozen

Germans who rushed to cut these down. Now a steady, if somewhat disorganised, stream of men came up the brows because *Daffodil* had pushed *Vindictive* firmly alongside. The ferryboat's seamen demolition parties with 22 Marines had to scramble over her bow to cross *Vindictive* in getting ashore. As the men came up they found Arthur Chater and the Sergeant-Major 'just as cool as if they were on parade' – organising the men. Some nevertheless waited a precious 10 minutes on the walkway before there was space for them on the ladders. Individuals used their own initiative, reassured by the Pom-Pom still firing from *Vindictive*'s fighting-top. There was less answering fire and Arthur Chater felt that there was none now hitting the top of brows, two more of which had been lowered onto the wall.

Men were still being killed on the ships, and as *Vindictive* was out of her intended position, her stern guns could not engage the seaward batteries. Lt-Cdr A. L. Harrison RN, knocked unconscious before the storming parties went ashore, recovered. Despite a broken jaw he went up a brow to lead the seamen along the walkway. They had orders to stay up there, clear of the Marines' attack being mounted along the mole's roadway, but the seamen had over 250m of exposed walkway to cross. German machine guns caught them in this daring rush – the walkway was little more than two metres wide – and the Commander was killed, but their Lewis gun which had killed the Germans attacking the ladders, now was used on the crews of the six 90-mm along the mole's tip. These guns did not then fire some minutes later when the blockships passed into the harbour. The inventive Wing-Cmdr F. A. Brock RAF had earlier sprinted along this walkway, dropped grenades into the lookout post near the 90-mm battery and was last seen climbing to examine a new type of German range-finder on the lookout's roof.

On the roadway Marines had been told to move out of the shed, and indeed the enemy's own shellfire was doing it more damage than the seamen's demolitions were likely to do. Arthur Chater had discussed the situation with Capt E. Bamford, commanding B Company, under the cover of No. 3 Shed with its raised solid floor intersected by channels for loading carts. Then at 12.20 am there was a blinding roar of an explosion from the shore end of the mole. The old submarine C3 had been driven under the piers of the viaduct linking the stonework of the mole to the shore – or rather: which *had* linked them. Some 5 tonnes of amatol on a 5-minute fuse had blown a 30m gap in the viaduct.

The rattle and reverberations of this explosion had hardly died away when Capt Bamford came across to the men who had come out of No. 3 Shed. A calm 'Fall in, B Company' and the men, 16 of them, began marching out towards a second battery of three 120-mm guns at the seaward end of the road. The Adjutant and Capt Bamford had changed the plan, as B Company's intended role of clearing the roadway *towards* the shore, was now less important than attacking the second seaward battery, and C Company, whose role this was, had virtually been destroyed. Out in the open more men joined the second column. They had to cross over 200m of 'flat pavement devoid of any cover', before reaching the trenches and wire defending the '120' battery.

A siren had been wailing for some minutes by 12.40, this was not the tooted morse 'K' as previously arranged for an emergency recall. Arthur Chater, therefore, went back aboard to confirm the ship was to sail, she was. (The siren was *Daffodil's* for *Vindictive's* had been shot away.) The Marines had expected to be ashore another 35 minutes and there were still bomb dumps, seaplane sheds and stores to be demolished, but far too few survivors to achieve this. Chater went back to the wall, calling and signalling with his arm to Capt Bamford and others to bring back the men to the ladders. Cpl Kingshott and Pte A. G. Clarke RMLI had reached a point overlooking the outer

battery, they confirmed it was no longer firing. No. 11 Platoon's few survivors with No. 12 had been to the left along the walkway, when the seamen needed reinforcements. They had reached the end of the walk, where it overlooked the battery on the 120-mm guns and the six 90-mm guns spaced along the outmost arm of the mole. Here they were at first checked by machine gun fire from the defended area below them, but coming down some steps they reached the first 90-mm to find it still under its covers. (There had been some Germans, therefore, who had not reached their action stations.) As No. 12 Platoon came back to the gangways, others reached the bottom of the ladders. Heavy shell fire was now coming down on the mole from many of the 144 coast batteries ashore, drawing fire which might have been more usefully directed at the blockships.

In this thickening hail of shell fragments, Arthur Chater remained by the ladders, directing the small numbers of each platoon up to the gangways. Capt C. P. Tuckey stayed at the foot of these the only escape routes, helping the men – many carrying wounded comrades – up the dangerous side of the wall, until he was killed. Lt Cooke (No. 5 Platoon), wounded for a second time, was brought in by his Marine Officer's Attendant (batman) who as the platoon's runner had also been hit. Some were less fortunate, the 16 men covering the final move across the road were captured; but No. 9 Platoon (Lt Lamplough, a future Major-General) covered the last few men to reach the couple of remaining ladders. The last Lewis gunner then withdrew as shell splinters wrecked his gun before he went down the gangway. By now Arthur Chater, 'could see no more men approaching' before going to report to the *Vindictive's* captain.

Vindictive let slip her mooring grapples and making heavy smoke 'almost asphyxiating those on deck', avoided any further shell-fire. The ferryboat, *Iris*, was not so fortunate; her attempts to land the A

(Chatham) Company had been frustrated. Coming alongside the mole ahead of *Vindictive*, two naval officers had been killed trying to secure her grapples to the wall. This prevented her mooring and using scaling ladders, so her First Lieutenant, the Captain having been mortally wounded, took her alongside *Vindictive* but the withdrawl was about to begin. As the little *Iris* moved away from the cruiser's side, she was exposed briefly but fatally to the shore guns' fire, for her smoke equipment failed. A hit near the bridge killed the ever cheerful Maj C. E. Eagles DSO, commander of the A Company, seven of his officers and 69 men, 105 were wounded (some earlier in the action). As coastal motorboats sped to lay a protective smoke screen, a fire started on the upper deck. The Corporal Bugler, L/Cpl C. Heffernan, moved nearby ammunition and was killed as he probably ditched some over the side.

The *Vindictive* was so heavily damaged that the stokers could see stars through great holes in her deck, but the ship could still make 17 knots despite this, and there was now time to take a welcome respite. Arthur Chater collected his fleece-lined Burberry from the signal bridge, it had been tattered by shell splinters. His knee was now 'very painful, as the danger from the enemy diminished', he had been hit probably when the CO was killed, but in the urgency of action had not noticed the wound. The cruisers' 6-in (150-mm) had fired until she was almost alongside the mole, but all the crew of the 7.5-in (190-mm) howitzer fitted forward had been killed as the ship came out of the smoke. Capt R. A. Dallas Brooks (a future Commandant General) took a seaman's gun crew to man it but they were all casualties before they could get the howitzer into action. The Captain went aft and found Sgt F. J. Knill maintaining a steady rate of fire with the 11-in (279-mm) howitzer, although half choked by German gas shells. (A third howitzer, a 7.5-in amidship, had shell-splinter damage and did not fire until the withdrawal.) The

howitzers bombarded shore batteries near the lock gates of the canal, and 12 very different Stokes guns were also manned on the bow and the boat deck, four of their crews from the RMA.

The fighting-top was a shambles, parts of the 'mattresses' shot away and the two Pom-Poms and four Lewis guns scarred by shell-splinters, the Lewis barrels ripped open in long jagged gashes. As *Vindictive* moved against the mole, the Marine gunners had kept the Germans' heads down, although spotting their positions was difficult. Then two shells in quick succession burst on this foretop, killing or wounding all its crew. Sgt Norman Finch had his right arm shattered but with his good arm kept one Pom-Pom in action until another shell wounded him further. The damage elsewhere on the ship was extensive, her wooden decks had been flooded keeping down the fire risk, and were now covered with a dangerous film of flame-thrower fuel for both these devices on the port side had been shot to pieces. There were many wounded, one old Marine bugler had a leg hanging on to his thigh by the sinew. Seamen used what dressing they could find – a shell having exploded in the sick bay – to patch him up using tourniquets. 'In this rather unpleasant business' they had to cut off his leg with a knife.

The objectives had been partly achieved in so far as the three blockships, the crews bravely staying with them as they steamed across the harbour under fire, were positioned and blocking the ship canal. The captain of *Vindictive* had seen *Thetis* wedge herself across the Channel but *Intrepid* and *Iphigenia* were in the canal, before he ordered the sounding of the recall siren. Only shallow-drafted vessels could move out within four days, and three weeks' dredging was needed to open a new channel. Six months later several German U-boats were found still in their camouflaged sheds and apparently had been trapped there since 23 April. Also, although the 4th Battalion had been unable to demolish many of the installations,

A 15-inch (381mm) howitzer of the RMA Howitzer Brigade in action on the Western Front in 1917. These were semi-mobile and could be dismantled to be moved to new positions; each of the ten guns with the Brigade had eleven trucks, two or three of which were towed together by special 100-hp tractors. Painting by R. French, RM Poole.

the Germans' own fire (as mentioned earlier) did much of this for them. The Battalion had 119 killed, 234 wounded and 13 missing (mostly prisoners), and as a mark of respect for their bravery there has never been another 4th RM Battalion.

Vindictive had returned to Dover to a great reception but some anxiety for *Iris* had not returned. She limped in at 2.45 pm, $10\frac{1}{2}$ hours after *Vindictive* and the sad job of burying the many dead began. They and the survivors received many justly deserved honours: Capt Carpenter RN,

Capt E. Bamford RMLI, Lt-Cdrs G. N. Bradford, A. L. Harrison, G. H. Drummond and R. Bourke, Lieutenants R. D. Sandford, V. A. C. Crutchley, and P. T. Dean of the Navy, Sgt N. A. Finch RMA, and Able Seaman A. E. McKenzie received the Victoria Cross. The whole battalion, not just the officers had voted for Captain Bamford's award and when it was found that an award for other ranks was also to be made, Sgt Finch was nominated.

The purpose in blocking the Bruges canal had been not only to trap U-boats,

they had penetrated over 60km to reach the outskirts of Amiens; the RMLI Battalions lost 772 all ranks, many of whom were wounded and taken prisoner, in a fighting retreat. After this crisis, German attacks on the Ypres salient also had some success in April, advancing their line over 15km by the end of the month. (A staggering comparison to the 300 to 400m of the British advance the previous year.) The raid at Zeebrugge, therefore, came at a time when the Allies needed some boost to their morale, and although not mounted for this purpose, the raid was just the tonic they required.

Later that summer – when the RMLI battalions were losing as many men in a morning's attack as were lost on the mole at Zeebrugge – the German offensive lost its momentum. Then, on 8 August, 'the black day of the German army in the history of war', began a British offensive which had such a demoralising effect on the Germans north of Amiens that: 'It unhinged the minds and morale of the German high command.' (The remaining RMLI Battalion by this time was training for open warfare.) It is difficult in purely military terms to see why this well executed and famous victory, 'the most brilliant gained by British arms' in World War I, should be decisive. Yet there is no doubt that the sweeping success to which it contributed – the armistice was signed 12 weeks later – points out how national morale becomes the dominant factor in major wars. The British navy, in Liddell Hart's words, 'was to win no Trafalgar' yet its blockade was decisive for the Germans were half starved and with ever worsening morale on the home front, they could not sustain a military offensive in the west. While for the Allies, the coming support of the Americans was another decisive factor, in terms of morale as much as men and war material.

Much has been written about the unfortunate generalship and staff work of World War I. For example at Passchendaele in October 1917, even if Haig's attacks of attrition had absorbed German

but also prevent the Germans freely using the large ship repair yards in this inland port. Using it had saved nearly 500km on the voyage to repair yards in Germany, which could be critical, for in the early months of 1918 the losses to the U-boat fleet were mounting and in May 14 were sunk out of the 125 in service, but on the Western front the Germans were scoring victories. A month before the Royal Marines and seamen stormed Zeebrugge, 'a German flood [of troops] inundated 40 miles of the British front'. By 28 March

Royal Marine Commando

Brigadier-General Frederick W. Lumsden VC, DSO and two bars. He was awarded the VC for gallantry while commanding a battalion of the Highland Light Infantry – he led artillery horse teams and a party of infantry to bring into the British lines six German field guns captured 300m forward of the British main positions in April 1917. He was awarded two bars to his DSO while commanding the 14th Brigade in the 32nd Division from 13 April 1917 until he was killed in the front line on 3 June 1918. Painting by A. Durrant Smyth, CGRM.

reserves, there would have been no strategic gain, since a breakthrough at that time in the north-west would not have seriously disrupted the flow of supplies to German armies to the south, facing French troops at a low ebb in their fortunes. In committing themselves to such land battles, it can be argued that the British had neglected their traditional use of amphibious forces, when a small and well-trained force could strike at vital enemy communications – an action which might gain a strategic advantage out of all proportion to the size of the force committed. (In France by 1917 the British armies totalled 1.2 million men, yet the French had 2.6 million and with their other allies the Franco-British armies would put nearly 4 million men against the German's 2.5 million.)

Whether or not the British might wish to continue a largely amphibious strategy, their continental partners in World War II and later years have expected a major British commitment to land forces. For the Marines immediately after World War I as for the whole of the Royal Navy, this was largely a matter for the future. The Marines went back to sea service with

naval gunnery as their chief role, but with a considerable experience of infantry fighting. Arthur Chater, Charles Lamplough and Dallas Brooks were but three of several young officers who later rose to the rank of General in the Corps. Robert Neville, who had served both at Jutland and in France was to be on the staff of Combined Operations by 1943 and later a Major General. While the Naval Staff Operations Officer of the Mediterranean fleet in 1915, William Godfrey, was Adjutant General from 1936 until retiring through ill-health three years later.

As these young officers rose to senior ranks, they appreciated the difficulties faced by most of their predecessors, who had never commanded a larger formation than a detachment. Although Maj Gen Archibald Paris, who had commanded the Royal Naval Division in the summer of 1916 until he was badly wounded that October, had commanded a 'flying column' in the Boer War. The Corps in 1939 would be, nevertheless, short of senior officers with experience of commanding large land forces.

In 1919 the RM Field Force[6] with 200 trained skiers, had been fighting in North Russia since the previous summer. This small force, with never more than 360 men in action, successfully created the impression of much greater strength, although their posts along the Murmansk railway were as far apart as Plymouth and Portsmouth or Boston and New York. In July their part in these little known operations was taken over by the 6th Battalion RMLI.[1] This battalion, with orders to keep losses to a minimum, fought several actions against Bolshevik forces and their Finnish allies. This campaign, however, had little popular support in Britain, although fought under the direction of the Supreme War Council of the Allies based in France.

Other Marines were involved in Allied campaigns at this time. In Siberia the detachment from HMS *Kent* had two 6-in (152-mm) naval guns and four 12-pounders mounted in a large Russian tug and barges.

These operated on the Kama River, nearly 10,000km west of Vladivostok, the Marines' base. During the early summer of 1919, they sank three armed Soviet steamers, frequently engaged in duels with Soviet artillery batteries and – until the Czech Legion withdrew – were efficiently supporting anti-Bolshevik forces. These 'fell apart' in late June and the Marine gunners began a long – if not the Corps' longest – withdrawal.

They dismantled their guns, meanwhile with local help extending a light railway line to the river. From there the 8 tonne 6-in guns were manoeuvred onto trucks, although there was only a 5.5-tonne crane available. (This lifted one 'end' onto a truck before the second could be lifted.) Seventy women then helped to manhandle the trucks to the mainline station, alongside the light railway. Trolleys broke through the light railway lines, and wedges had then to be found to chock them up while the line was repaired. At last the mainline trucks (of an armoured train) were loaded from the trolleys, an engine 'found' and over 15 tonnes of ammunition and stores put in wagons as well as the six guns. The railway officials were loath to part with their engine but the train left Perm (on the Kama River) at 6 am on the morning of 29 June. Tranship-ping the guns from the river boats to the armoured train had been achieved in three

days, despite the chaotic conditions in the town.

The Marines reached Omsk, where there was the possibility of using the guns in support of the local forces, but the Admiralty decided to withdraw them. A few days before they left Omsk, 250 people had been hurt in one train of the many the Bolsheviks wrecked. But the Marines 'were prepared to deal with any opposition we were likely to meet'. This included the ravages of cholera and other

Above: Marines of HMS *Suffolk* with one of her 6-inch (152mm) guns on a railway truck during their journey from Vladivostok to west of Omsk, a distance of nearly 1,000km. They had been landed in the autumn of 1918 and were relieved by a detachment from HMS *Kent* in March 1919.

Left: L/Cpl Walter R. Parker VC, RMLI was awarded the VC for extreme courage as a stretcher bearer at Gallipoli on 30 April and 1 May 1915. Painting by G. H. Downing, RM Museum, Eastney.

Right: Capt Edward Bamford VC, DSO, RMLI was awarded the VC by ballot from those who took part in the Zeebrugge landing in which his total disregard for danger showed a magnificent example to his men. Painting by W. J. Rowden, RM Museum, Eastney.

Above left: Sgt Norman A. Finch VC, RMA was awarded the Victoria Cross for his valuable work in *Vindictive*'s foretop during the landing on the mole at Zeebrugge. Painting by G. H. Downing, RM Museum, Eastney.

Above right: Major Francis J. W. Harvey, VC, RMLI was awarded the Victoria Cross for presence of mind and devotion to duty when mortally wounded after an explosion in 'Q' turret of HMS *Lion* during the Battle of Jutland, 31 May 1916.

Bottom: One of the 12-inch (152mm) guns installed by RM gunners to cover the Dardanelles from the north shore during the British deployment in 1922 to deter Turkish nationalists from crossing the straits. These guns had an arc of fire covering over 45km of the southern shores of the straits near Chanak.

fevers, one Marine with smallpox being isolated behind a partition they built on one wagon, but this killer did not spread. They passed through burnt-out railway stations, were delayed by wrecks (another with over 250 casualties), and were isolated for 48 hours in Harbin (Manchuria) due to cholera in the town's Chinese quarter, but on the 52nd day of this adventure they reached Vladivostok.

During the next two decades, Fleet Marines in China and battalions deployed in Ireland (1920–22), Turkey (1922–23) and Shanghai (1927), would be prepared for action if not in it. During these years also the Corps developed their skills with landing craft (albeit in experimental work only), in land artillery and a number of more unusual military ventures which maintained their versatility (see Appendix 2 and Note 7). This – always a key note in the Corps' approach to war – would be tested and proved nigh inexhaustible in the coming World War II.

Chapter 6

World War II: Green Beret and Landing Craft Actions

Three Skua fighter-bombers flew off the carrier HMS *Ark Royal* to answer an SOS on 14 September 1939: the SS *Fanad Head* was being shelled by a German submarine, U30, some 650km south-west of Ireland. As Lt Guy B. K. Griffiths RM flew towards the action, he saw lifeboats in the water and gunfire from the U-boat trying to sink the ship. Diving to the attack, the air-gunner positioned behind Guy Griffiths braced himself for the expected surge as the Skua pulled out of the dive after the bomb was dropped. They could see swirling eddies around the U-boat as she crash-dived, but although their 112lb (460kg) anti-submarine bomb should have exploded beneath these, there was instead a sudden juddering explosion – the fuse was faulty – that blasted the tail plane. Guy Griffiths managed to raise the Skua's nose but without the tail she flopped forward onto the sea.

There was just time to slide back the cockpit cover above the pilot's seat, but the air gunner could not force open his rounded hatch. Lt Thurstan RN, diving with the second Skua, had the same trouble. His bomb also burst on the sea's surface and blew away the Skua's tail. Both pilots swam clear of the wreckage but the air gunners were lost, trapped in the planes which sank in seconds. They had ditched not far from *Fanad Head* to which they swam, clambering aboard up a rope ladder swinging from her side. They were safe for the moment, but the U-boat's conning tower broke the surface nearby, to the pilot's discomfort. A boat pulled away from the submarine and brought a search party aboard the ship, looking for the ship's papers. As U30 was

clearly going to sink *Fanad Head* once these were found, the pilots allowed themselves to be captured. This was 11 days after war had been declared by the British in what became World War II.

Guy Griffiths later took part in the first attempt to escape by tunnelling out of the Dulag Luft POW Camp in 1940, but was not to succeed. In May 1945, over $5\frac{1}{2}$ years after he was captured, he was finally released from a Prisoner-Of-War Camp in Hungary. During these years the Corps had undertaken many new roles, and expanded to 78,400 by 1944 (see Chap. 4, Note 4). From the battle of the River Plate in December 1939 when RM gunners were in action aboard *Exeter*, *Ajax* and *Achilles*, Marines would play their part in naval actions throughout this war: including battles fought through Arctic seas escorting convoys to Murmansk and past the gauntlet of Axis bombers to Malta. Their guns were in the invasion bombardments of North Africa, Sicily, the Salerno beachhead, the landings in Normandy and actions half a world away with the British Pacific Fleet.

On land the first Marines units in action were in Norway (April–May 1940) where they also had a few landing craft. At this time Royal Marine anti-aircraft gunners helped to defend Britain in the early days of the 'Blitz' and by 1944 there was an RM Anti-Aircraft Brigade of 3,000 Marines with 22,000 Army personnel. The RM (Amphibious) Brigade formed in December 1939 was held for special operations, went to Dakar (French West Africa) in the summer of 1940 and would later provide men for the RM Commandos, after the number of battalions had been increased

RM gun-mounting teams and landing craft companies put ashore heavy guns for the defence of naval bases. Here a 3.7-inch (94mm) anti-aircraft gun with its cradle and pedestal are being loaded onto Motor Landing Craft No. 18, a forerunner of the later mechanised landing craft.

Viper' on the Irrawaddy during the retreat from Burma in February 1942. One of the MNBDO infantry battalions had heavy losses in an unsuccessful raid on Tobruk in September 1942; others became landing craft crews, manning the guns of major support craft from 1942 and two-thirds of the British assault craft on the Normandy beaches in June 1944. RM Commandos had landed at Dieppe in 1942 and by June 1944 there were nine of these units each with over 450 men: five fought in north-west Europe; two in Italy and Dalmatia aiding partisans; and two in the Far East.

The many operations of these forces are summarised in Note 1, but some Royal Marines took part in almost every major action at sea and many ashore. For instance, Marines flew with the Fleet Air Arm, there were Royal Marine Engineers clearing enemy harbours as soon as these were captured, some were in the Army Commandos formed in June 1940, some were raiders with the Special Boat Squadron and the Marines' own 'Cockleshell' heroes of the RM Boom Patrol Detachment. Unit titles were deliberately misleading and few people in 1945 knew that men of 'Detachment 385' were canoeists, often landed by flying boat for clandestine missions in Japanese occupied Malaya. The variety of roles is almost endless: an RM major operated Chinese guerrillas out of Java; a few Marines were trained coast watchers in touch with Cairo General Headquarters from their hideouts in Mediterranean islands; and Sir Winston Churchill chose Royal Marines for his personal bodyguard. The Marines included in their ranks: pilots, deep-sea and shallow water divers, artillerymen and naval gunners, commandos and members of the Special Operation Executive's clandestine forces, as well as the more usual military skills of, for example, infantryman and signaller. Those who served with this last qualification were not only trained in army procedures but also in naval ones, in a typical example of the dual roles *per mare, per terram* of all Marines.

to form three brigades in the RM Division. (This amphibious assault division should not be confused with the 'Port' HQ Divisions.) The Mobile Base Defence Organisations (MNBDOs) of which there were two, had been formed in 1939 and 1940 from the nucleus of men trained to install coast and other guns in naval advanced bases.

The Marines of one MNBDO helped build the seafire defences along the south coast of England, and men of this Boom Scaffolding Unit also flew hydrogen balloons trailing steel wires to drift across German overhead power cables. The MNBDOs would provide not only such unusual units, but also some MNBDO coast-gunners formed the special 'Force

Much of their versatility stemmed from sea service, one example of the many must, however, suffice from these years of the 'rough, tough history of the Royal Marines', as Sir Winston Churchill once described it. Ronald ('Tubby') Healiss was a fuse-setter in a 4.7-in gun's crew on the aircraft carrier HMS *Glorious*. She was returning from Narvik (Norway) and still north of the Arctic Circle in the late afternoon of 8 June 1940, when she was caught by *Scharnhorst*, whose salvo of shells hit the carrier's flight deck. Smoke spilled over into the gun position for the hangar was afire and soon took hold with a red wall of flame that roared up behind Tubby Healiss's gun position. There were no orders coming to the gunners and as a

second salvo hit they used their initiative and moved up to the flight deck. There, however, they could do nothing for the petrol fires were beyond control. Nor could they get near the fires in the lower hangar, although they went below to try to put them out.

The ship was listing as they came back 'up top', and it was a long drop as Tubby went over the side. 'There was a whirling impression of green and black' as he came up to the surface, half unconscious from his belly-flop dive. He had taken off his duffle coat, seaboots and jacket before he dived and the suction as he surfaced had stripped him of trousers and seaboot stockings. He quickly blew more air into his lifejacket as the intense cold gripped

A 3.7-inch (94mm) howitzer of the RM Light Battery in Norway, April 1940. They were landed at Namsos from a destroyer but were chosen by Army HQ, for their discipline and high morale, to serve as infantry in the rearguard that covered the evacuation.

him, for the water temperature was only 5°C. His dive had brought him clear of the still churning propellors, and near to a canvas air cushion. This he clung to with three others, brushing oil from their eyes. The sea had been glass calm but was becoming choppy, making some men sick. They weakened and lost their grip on flotsam to float away and drown.

Tubby Healiss swam 50m to what turned out to be one of the ship's damaged motor-boats, strong arms pulled him aboard. Oil, the cold and exposure to the sea began to take their toll, as the men tried to keep awake with a singsong and games of tombola (the naval equivalent of bingo), but they dozed off even in the perpetual daylight of the Arctic summer. By midnight only five were still alive. The Surgeon-Commander who had taken charge of the boat ordered Tubby to cut the dead from their lashings, and next morning he saw the last body sink slowly behind the transom and was now alone.

Much later two dots appeared on the horizon and his boat drifted towards them. They were life rafts, Carley floats,

with men on them. He decided to swim across to join them, first deflating his life-jacket so he would go down quickly if cramp paralysed him. He cut the lifeline, picked a blue patch of sky 'over' the rafts and swam towards it.

His progress was slow but steady although 'first the feet, then the calves, the knees and the thighs grew stiff'. There was an almost intolerable pain in his stomach as he rose and fell with each wave, but he reached the rafts. 12 hours had passed since he had spoken to anyone, but his new companions made him welcome. There were 50 men on these rafts during the second night after sinking, but next day only a Petty Officer and Tubby were still alive. After several vain attempts to attract the attention of aircraft, they saw a trawler – whales had been spouting all morning and at first they mistook its plume of smoke for another jet of spume. The fishermen had seen them, however, and hauled them to safety, two of some 37 survivors – 1,515 men of *Glorious* and her two escort destroyers had been lost.

There were to be other enemy victories,

RM gunners in a 15-inch (381mm) turret of the battleship HMS *Malaya*, which covered Atlantic and Malta convoys, bombarded Genoa in February 1941 and served in the Eastern Fleet in 1944. Royal Marines manned at least one turret in the main armament of capital ships and cruisers, as well as part of their secondary armament, from the 1890s to the 1950s.

and Royal Marines knew the bitterness of defeat. On Crete a rearguard of over 400 Royal Marines held the last defence line, covering the evacuation which ended in the early hours of 1 June 1941. When the Allies were withdrawing before Japanese armies, RM Coast gunners formed a special river force in February 1942. Known as 'Force Viper' – for it was intended 'to bite the enemy hard' – these Marines supported the British and Indian troops retreating northward in Burma. The launches of the Force were used to ferry men to demolition and patrol work along the Irriwaddy; and from their smaller boats they made several suicidal attacks on Japanese approaching river crossings.

At Dieppe, six months later, men of the RM Commando landed 'with a courage terrible to see'. They had been intended as a cutting out force to capture German landing craft, but in the event were put ashore in support of Canadian Infantry. Due to misunderstandings at the force HQ, afloat off the beaches, the landing was made in the teeth of enemy fire. The Commando CO, Lt-Col J. P. Phillipps RM, saw the impossibility of his men surviving in this hurricane of enemy fire, as the craft came clear of their smoke screen. With a complete disregard of the enemy's fire, he stood high on the wheelhouse roof of his LCM and signalled the following craft back into the smoke before he was killed. By his bravery he had saved the lives of 200 of his men, but RM casualties at Dieppe were 247 including those in the guns' crews of major supporting craft.

These major craft were landing craft (LCTs) adapted to carry anti-aircraft Oerlikons and Pom-Poms as LC Flak ships

Cruisers of Admiral Vian's Mediterranean Squadron break clear of their smoke screen to attack the Italian battleship *Littorio* and her escorts north of the Gulf of Sirte on 22 March 1942. On board each cruiser was a detachment of 80–100 Marines and RM Bandsmen, the musicians manned the ships' gunnery controls. Painting by Norman Wilkinson, National Maritime Museum, London.

Above: A Ju52 on fire over Heraklion, Crete after being hit by anti-aircraft fire in May 1941. RM gunners manned a battery in the port's AA defences. *Below:* An RM launch from Force 'Viper' covering demolitions on the Irrawaddy in March 1942.

(LCFs) or two 4.6-in (119-mm) naval guns in open gunhouses as LC Guns (Large). They were in action in daylight for the first time at Dieppe, closing the beaches regardless of the risks from mortar and heavier fire. LCF No. 2, going into point-blank range of the German defences, gave close support to the men ashore until – her Captain, Lt E. L. Graham, RNVR, killed – the Oerlikons and Pom-Poms were put out of action one by one. She finally sank and only a few survivors were rescued from the sea. (The Royal Marine Commando was rebuilt after these losses and designated 40 RM Commando in October 1942, by which date 41 RM Commando had been formed. '41 RM' was formed from 8th RM Battalion that month, which set the pattern for the formation of further RM Commandos (see Appendix 2). The Army had formed the first Commandos in June 1940, at a time when the Royal Marine Brigades were being held for possible operations in Ireland, should the Germans invade there. When on 23 June 1940 men of the Independent Companies, fore-runners of the Commandos, raided beaches near Boulogne on the French coast. From this small beginning, these Army Commandos had become by August 1942 a formidable – if relatively small – force.)

3 Commando, caught in the fire of a German convoy off Dieppe, nevertheless put 18 men commanded by Maj Peter Young, Bedfordshire and Hertfordshire Regiment, 'shore-sides' of the coast battery east of Dieppe, some 30 minutes before the main landings. Their fire was sufficient to

distract the German gunners who did not hit any of the approaching ships, these being hidden by smoke before the men of 3 Commando withdrew. On the western flank at this time Lord Lovat's 4 Commando carried out a classic operation successfully to destroy the German coast battery also before the time of the main landings. This battery's role had included a barrage of defensive fire off Dieppe's sea front, but its 150-mm guns were silenced after 4 Commando's attack.

In the Mediterranean that September a complex operation was mounted against Tobruk. In this, Royal Marines of MNBDO I's 11th RM Battalion, attempted to seize this supply port but were repulsed in part due to assault craft breakdowns on a large-scale – taking over 220 casualties. An earlier plan had proposed carrying out this raid with a small force, which might have been more successful, although German agents had forewarned their defences of the raid.

Certainly destroying fast blockade runners at Bordeaux 112km up the Gironde from the French Atlantic coast needed a small force. The alternative was to land two divisions with heavy air cover, inevitably leading to many civilian casualties. Therefore five two-man canoes of the Royal Marine Boom Patrol Detachment set off on the night of 7 December 1942 from the submarine *Tuna*. Two canoes successfully planted their limpet mines on several ships four days later, so that the Japanese would not get their cargoes of the latest German fuses and radar equipment.

There were only two survivors of this raid, who came out along one of the French Resistance's escape routes. The other eight 'Cockleshell' heroes were either drowned or shot while prisoners of war. But the main tide of the war was beginning to flow against the Axis when marine gunners in big ships and the major support craft covered the 'Torch' North African landings that November. In July 1943 40 and 41 RM Commandos landed on the flanks of British assault beaches in Sicily, and 7th RM Battalion organised the build-up of supplies in one beach area. After which this Battalion was sent forward into the line and were in action at the crossing of the Dittaino river.

At Salerno, Italy, in September, 41 RM and 2 (Army) Commandos were in almost continuous action for over a week, suffering 50% casualties. There were other Commando operations in the Mediterranean theatre[1] including those in support of partisans on the Dalmation islands. Here on Brac on 1–2 June 1944, '43' and '40' had a difficult assault against well entrenched German positions. And although they captured a key defence stronghold they were unable to hold it. Having cut their way through wire,

A Bren gun carrier of 11th RM Battalion crosses a Ceylonese beach at speed in 1943. This battalion formed part of the island's defences against expected Japanese raids.

Right: P Troop of 41 RM Commando receive a final inspection before their assault on Punta di Castellazo in the invasion of Sicily on 10 July 1943.

Below: An LC Gun (large) with its two 4.7-inch (119mm) guns in open gunhouses supports partisans in the Adriatic in 1945.

crossed minefields and charged concrete strong points with stones heaped around them for added protection on one ridge, the Germans successfully counter-attacked '43'. Later when '40' gained this hill, enemy fire from other strong points forced them to retreat.

The campaign in Italy was deprived of landing craft for amphibious operations in order to build up the invasion fleets for Normandy. For these the Corps, ever versatile, remustered men from the battalions – not all of whom had the physique to be commandos – from the MNBDOs and other units to become landing craft crews. They, by the autumn of 1943, formed flotillas of LC Assault, LC Mechanised and LC Personnel (Large), some 10,000 being trained in little over six months. This switch from land to sea service met the British strategic need for a large additional force of 'seamen'. By 1945, however, Pacific operations would be mounted by major craft on which the 'cargo' personnel could live during comparatively long voyages, therefore minor craft were no longer required in great numbers. The need in 1945 was for infantry to finish the war in Europe, and Royal Marines of the landing craft flotillas then formed two infantry brigades.

The assault craft (LCAs) were carried aboard such Landing Ships as HMS *Glenearn*. She had been converted originally from a 19-knot cargo ship to carry LCAs for the army commandos, and sailed in operations in the Mediterranean before being given a major refit in the winter of 1943 after which she embarked Royal Marine flotillas: 12 LCA of '535' and the same number of '543', she also carried three LCM. These latter were launched by derrick-cranes, but the LCAs had special davits, the craft being lowered on pulley ropes (falls) and unhooked as soon as they reached the water. After sailing from Portsmouth on the evening of 5 June 1944, through channels cleared in the mine fields, those on deck about 3.30 am saw the flashes of Allied bombs on the horizon. The drone of planes overhead – glider borne troops heading for Normandy, the crews later learnt – and the flicker of distant 'flak' foreshadowed a lively landing.

The LC crews and the assault companies which they would land – men of the 2nd East Yorks and South Lancs – breakfasted at about 4.30 am. Thirty minutes later, as the first streaks of light appeared, the troops began to buckle on their equipment. The LC crews clambered to their

A Centaur tank of No. 4 Battery of the RM Armoured Support Group, which had landed with the assault companies on D-Day, 6 June 1944. The tanks' 95mm (3.7-inch) gun-howitzers gave close support to forward troops in the next three weeks.

stations, before the first 10 craft were swung down to the levels of the loading decks and the crews climbed aboard. At this time the troops were marshalled by Platoons, each of three Sections, ready to cross gangways. When the Marine cox'n (coxswain) gave the platoon commander the word, he took his men over and into the stern of the LCA and they filed forward. Three lines of men, the outboard two sitting under the protection of the LCA's armoured sidedecks, the centre Section crouched on the low seating 'planks' along the LCA's floor. Despite the wires holding the LCA to a fender, the craft swayed with the motion of the ship. But in practice landings by these LCAs with the platoons now loading, the drills had been perfected. Men with lengths of Bangalore Torpedo (for cutting paths in wire), a sergeant with the extra bulky load of fuses hung on his gear, and the nervous, all were safely loaded.

'Boat manned' the cox'n called to the telephone operator at the loading station, which he reported to the 'LC' Control Room. A cox'n then reminded the Pongos – a soldier is affectionately known to Marines as Percy Pongo – to 'look up, 'cos the pulleys at the ends of falls fore and aft, will thrash about a bit when we hit the water'. And this they do, as the sea is rising and falling a metre or more. Nevertheless all the craft unshackled the falls and floated free, except one. The after falls of the pioneer platoon's LCA were jammed and the craft tilted alarmingly to 45°. The cox'n kept his head, calming the passengers, while seamen worked to free the falls.

LCA 994 (Lt Webber RM) moved off from the towering side of the ship, and possible danger of damage as the craft rose against this steel wall was past – '994' moving to circle off the starboard bow as the second flight of eight craft were being lowered. Within 15 minutes all 12 craft of 535 Flotilla were afloat. Three kilometres to the east, the battleship *Warspite* was bombarding Villerville coast battery, two of her three 15-in turrets manned by Marines (the fourth turret was out of action). Only occasional shells from this and other German batteries fell near the growing armada of craft; but *Glenearn's* crew had seen a Norwegian destroyer explode amidships and the bow come up to meet her stern like the closing of a giant jack-knife.

The 536 RM Flotilla's 18 LCAs, launched from *Empire Cutlass*, joined *Glenearn's* craft and the South Lancs and East York's assault companies were set for the beach. The LCAs took station between columns of LC Tank carrying the assault vehicles of the Royal Engineers, AVREs and two LCT (Armoured) carrying Royal Marine tanks. All was going to plan, although in the rough water the cox'ns had a job keeping station, yet there were over 12km to go, with only 80 minutes to cover them. Water bounced in over the forward ramp, but behind the LCAs armoured doors the Yorkshires were comparatively safe.

Some 2km from the beach the LCTs came line abreast, and the columns of LCAs came on, their position checked by a destroyer on the flank. There the LC Gun (Large) No. 9 fired at shore targets, her Marines sweating to get up ammunition. The tank crews in an LCT(A), water slopping in the well around the two Centaurs, fired at one strong point. They were finding 'targets of opportunity' now, although their OC – out of his Sherman and on the LCT's bridge – had difficulty in spotting these. Two large buildings could be identified in the panoramic air photograph, the LCT's skipper confirming their position. Shells and mortar bombs were falling among the craft and the flank destroyers responded. One LCA, a mortar bomb falling on her stern deck, quickly became a mass of flames.

In the LCAs not only the soldiers were feeling seasick, but if the anti-sickness pills were not much help, a mug of tea worked wonders even though it was salted with spray. The insulated tea 'bucket' behind the LCA bowman's armoured position was indeed an inspiration. The soldiers were allowed to smoke and with discretion to stretch cramped legs, but with your head above the armoured side decks, the whirling shrapnel and clip of machine gun fire seemed very close. Yet there was just time to see the beach, or at least the dust pall beyond the water's edge. And the flashes of bursting shells – our's or their's? Who could tell? Aircraft came in low, the shore bombardment having lifted while they strafed the pill-boxes. These planes had hardly zoomed back to a safe height when a great whoosh and roar startled many in the LCAs. This was the naval LCT (Rocket)s laying a pattern of explosive warheads some 680m long, to explode mines and cut wire where the assault companies would break through the defences. A few of 592 RM Flotilla's LCA (Hedgerow) with their spigot mortars also fired and turned away. They had suffered in the heavy seas while under tow behind LCTs and now the few that did reach the coast – many had foundered – had difficulties.

As the last leaking LCA(HR) struggled clear of the LCA columns, in came three support craft. These had 6-pounder anti-tank guns with RM gunners in bow turrets of the type used in armoured cars. They fired at the machine gun cupolas on strong points and, with the destroyers, 'shot' in the LCAs so effectively that there was little direct fire at the Yorks and Lancs' craft until these were almost ashore. About 400m out, the flotilla leaders hoisted the flags 'deploy to port and starboard' – the stunted masts of these leading craft were difficult to see, but in good order '535' and '536' came into line for the final run-in. Each bowman slipped off the tackle holding the armoured bow doors, and tested the ramp to be sure it would drop. The beach was 200m away, and the LCA's engineer in the unarmoured stern used all possible power. They were early and the bombardment would not lift for several minutes, but there was no point in hanging about to give German gunners a clear shot.

At the bow, the ramp was lowered, and the Sections – centre first, port and star-board files together – were soon over it. The Yorkshiremen on *Sword* beach, ex-pecting a large white house, found they had been landed immediately opposite it, where the beach was sandy and flat. For a few minutes all was quiet after the naval bombardment lifted. The soldiers raced for the sand dunes, having waded waist deep in some cases to get ashore. The LCAs, equally anxious to quit the beach, hauled out to recover their kedges, manoeuvring between the 'sticks of Rom-mel's asparagus'. This collection of old shells on ramps pointing seaward and Teller mines on 2–3m poles, could – and did – blow the bows off an LCA. Mortar fire began falling along the tide line, but '535' got out with only four craft lost; others were less fortunate.

543 RM Flotilla, carrying the two follow-up companies and battalion HQ of the East Yorks joined up with eight LCAs of '538' from *Broadsword*. Their run to the beach followed that of '535' but they would land half an hour after the first flights. From ashore the assault companies radioed that despite increasing opposi-tion, they were making progress, the Yorkshire's colonel therefore asked the LCAs of '543' to slow their approach while for half a minute he scanned the beach with his binoculars. He identified the lighthouse at Ouistreham to the left, and satisfied they were heading for the right point to land, the LCAs increased speed. By now the tide covered many more obstacles, and only one 'lane' had been cut through these. '535' passed seaward, but the LCAs coming in began to queue, there would be no fast run over the last few hundred metres as cox'ns had to pick their way among the obstacles. They did not drop their kedges – causing LCA 1216 to broach-to – but instead felt their way in.

With them, in two of '535's' craft, were RN Beach Commandos and a party of RM shallow water divers, with explosives to clear obstacles: an LC Obstruction Clear-ance Unit (LCOCU). The onshore wind, however, causing the tide to flood early, made the water deeper than expected.

D-Day in Normandy, 6 June 1944. In the invasion, 16,000 Royal Marines took part as commandos, assault craft crews (one of their LCAs can be seen in the left centre) and in ships covering the invasion.

Royal Marine Commando

Lt O. W. Jackson RM's LCOCU laid marker buoys from the single channel off Red Beach, but craft were sailing between the obstacles, and they could not dive to clear them. Nevertheless 'tin hats on their heads' they cleared mines and obstacles at the water's edge.

Two craft who landed the seamen of 142 Beach Commando stayed near the shore to act as duty boats for the Beach Commander and his staff when the rest of the second flight began to withdraw. Their kedges were sometimes used to explode fused shells fixed to obstacles, but finding a route clear of them was difficult as many shells were completely submerged. By 9 am LCA 1216 had been almost an hour probing for a clear lane through the mines, when mortar fire from east of the beachhead began falling near the craft. One bomb hit the side decks of the well, wounding Lt Maton and his signaller. 'Water came pouring in' rising quickly as a second bomb burst forward, trapping the engineer in the tiny engine room and killing the signalman. However, the Lieutenant, the coxswain and the bow-man swam clear, their inflated life-belts keeping them afloat. Two LCMs coming out from off-loading vehicles they had put ashore, picked up these survivors. Three crews of '543' could not get off and after their craft were sunk, they made their way ashore. There they worked with parties clearing the beaches during the next few days. For the Marine LC crews, the second flights met the greatest opposition and all had more casualties on withdrawing than they suffered on the run-in.

Other Marines (some 16,000 were in the Normandy invasion landings) came ashore with 1 and 4 Commando Brigades to hold the Orne flank of the beachhead and capture other flank strongpoints. There were tank crews in the RM Armoured Support Group, crews of LCMs in the ferry service from stores ships to the beaches, radar plotters, VHF radio-telephone operators and other specialist signallers, RM Engineer clearance parties removing blockships and mines from the

harbours, RM Military Police – one sergeant being, so it seemed, the only man alive on *Sword* beach as he directed traffic – and there were a host of other jobs for them to do. Some, like bomb-disposal, were planned; others, like the salvaging of landing craft, which fell to the Marines of the Air Defence Section, illustrated the Marines' continuing adaptability.

The RM Commandos, here as elsewhere in World War II, spearheaded with Army Commandos the flank force assaults.[1] Or, in difficult terrain where tanks and heavy infantry found the going difficult, commandos were in the van of the Allied advance. Of the five RM Commandos landing on D-day 6 June 1944, 45 RM came ashore with 1 Commando Brigade on *Sword* beach, where this Brigade reinforced the scattered units of 6 Airborne Division on low hills east of the Orne. '45' – the '45th of Foot' as it is sometimes colloquially called today – had to cross 10km of enemy held territory with 3 and 6 Army Commandos. The Marines' CO was wounded, but they fought off German counter-attacks reaching the river and a canal intending to cross these in rubber boats but the bridges were intact.

This eastern flank was loosely held by commandos and paratroops for the next few hours, with '45' making a push northward back to the coast east of the river in order to disrupt German communications. They became isolated from the Brigade, fought their way back to the perimeter and later made further sallies against the German's stiffening resistance.

Meanwhile, 41 RM Commando on the right of *Sword* beach turned west. There was at least 5km between the landing beaches and '41' intended to forge the link with '48' landing on the left of *Juno* beach, but 41 Commando's LC Infantry (Small) were wooden craft with only light armour plate. Some craft came in nearly 300m further to the west flank than intended, and met heavy fire. Both commanders of the two Troops established ashore (a commando had five Troops)

were casualties, as were the Forward Observation Officers. The latter would have had radio links to the support craft and later to the mobile artillery, but without these there could be no controlled artillery support. The Troops' attack on a major coastal strongpoint near Lion-sur-Mer therefore stalled.

'48' had their difficulties in LCI(S) caught in deep water by 'Rommel's asparagus'. Several men were drowned trying to swim ashore, their Colonel was wounded but assembling his men in the dunes behind the beach led them over 900m inland. Here they established a firm base from which they attacked the rear of defended houses and the strong point at Langrune. This was a complex of houses with bricked up windows surrounded by anti-tank mines with a wide 2m-high wall blocking the only road here to the beach.

At the western flank of the British and Canadian assault, 47 RM Commando came inshore to find four tanks under fire at the most westerly landing point. They themselves had been under fire from 75mm guns for the last 2km of the run-in. Turning east, they took more casualties as the craft ran parallel to the coast before beaching among LCTs crowded together on *Gold* beach, 'drowned' vehicles, damaged assault craft and a Beach Master's nightmare of confusion. The Commando's craft were spread over 1,400m of tideline, not the planned 200m; some had been sunk, others snarled up on beach obstacles 300m from the shore at this point which was a long 'swim' with 40kg of kit or more if you were bringing ashore a Vickers MG barrel or the base plate of a 3-in mortar. Nevertheless, they struggled ashore, although the beach was not yet secured, and set off inland. Their objective was Port-en-Bessin which lay between the British and the *Omaha* landing points of the Americans, 10km to the west.

That night advanced units of German armoured forces probed the gap between

Men of 48 Commando dig-in among the wrecks of 6 Airborne Division's gliders near Pegasus bridge on 9 June 1944. The Commando had been in action on D-Day and would fight in the Orne line with other RM Commandos until the breakout in mid-August.

On 1 November 1944 4 Commando Brigade stormed the dykes of Walcheren in the Scheldt estuary. Many were landed in amphibians such as the Weasel in the picture that is followed by an LVT (Landing Vehicle tracked). The three RM Commandos (41, 47 and 48) had secured a beachhead and cleared the western dykes within two days of landing.

'41' and '48'. '47' were isolated, 6km to the west of the main perimeter, on a hill 'Point 72'. To the east '45' held an equally isolated point north-east of the main defences, but '46' were still at sea. Their proposed landing to take German batteries even further east had been cancelled, as these guns were not the major threat to shipping which they might have been. 46 RM Commando was therefore landed next day, replacing their demolition stores and close-range weapons with Canadian Bren guns, mortars and some German LMGs. That morning they cleared one of the last German coastal strong points, an area 350m by 140m with all-round defence including anti-tank guns. 46 Commando in the first week ashore fought several bold actions in support of the Canadians, and the other four Commandos were redeployed in the Orne line.

Although Commandos are trained for special operations, the Normandy build-up emphasised the need for them on occasions to fight as infantry. There was no-one to replace them during the five

weeks Marine and Army Commandos with airborne forces held the east flank. Aggressive patrolling, on almost inexhaustible stamina – especially during the first five days – and skill at arms, held off all German attempts to roll up the beachhead from the east. The rotting corpses in No-Man's Land, the cows needing milking, accurate German fire and 'hairy' raids are memories of these hot summer days. To the Germans the effects of naval fire support, 'this rapid firing artillery' as General Rommel called it, proved a decisive factor as 'any operation with infantry or armoured formations (became) impossible' in an area commanded by the naval guns, some tanks being destroyed up to 27km from the beach areas.

In August the Commando Brigades broke out of the beachhead, making long night infiltrations – 40km in stygian darkness, as in single-file men waded along beds of streams, climbed wooded slopes and crossed many fences. A trick not to be tried with inexperienced troops, for their weeks in Normandy had turned

the youngsters who had survived into hardened soldiers. Their casualties had been high: early in the landings '41' had suffered a 50% casualty rate, '45' about the same, '46' lost 60 men in one attack alone, '47' lost 200 at Port-en-Bessin, '48' had 220 casualties by the fifth day of the invasion, and all the Commandos' colonels had been wounded. By late August the Commandos were substantially under strength, yet retained their aggressive spirit, although much of the exuberance of the early days had gone.

Although the 1st Commando Brigade (designated with an ordinal for originally its men were drawn from the Guards Brigade) returned to the UK that autumn to retrain for operations in the Pacific, 4 Commando Brigade remained in France and by October were training with amphibious vehicles near Ostend (Belgium). They would land on 1 November across the shallows of the Scheldt estuary to seize Walcheren. This was defended by over 50 coast and heavy AA batteries, with ground defences manned by the German 70 Division, known as the 'White-bread' division, who had many men with gastric illnesses. 4 Army Commando (who replaced 46 RM's 260 men in 4 Brigade) landed from LCAs at Flushing on Walcheren's south coast, seized the town with the help of an Army infantry brigade and after four days of fierce street fighting, were established to the west of it. On the morning of 1 November the LCG(L)s, LCFs, LCT(R)s and two specially designed LCG (Medium) led in the assault by 4 Commando Brigade. The German batteries engaged these craft and in a series of duels which lasted for most of the morning, 16 of the 25 gunnery craft were sunk or put out of action. However, they had absorbed much of the German's fire, allowing 41, 47 and 48 RM Commandos to get ashore. '41' came ashore by a gap in the dykes, blown weeks earlier by over 250 bombers, near Westkapelle village. An RM LCOCU party landed first, but the old dyke wall some 20m high was too slippery for tracked vehicles to climb. The one Flail tank ashore here nevertheless reached

Men of 2 Commando Brigade advance across open country south of Comacchio in northern Italy. It was in this campaign that Corporal Tom Hunter won a posthumous Victoria Cross.

Right: RM commandos in an LC Assault craft cross the River Maas, Holland in 1945.

Below: 3 Commando Brigade, composed of two Army and two RM Commandos, move 20km up the Thegyan river in January 1945 to seize Hill 170 – a key position on the Japanese line of retreat from the Arakan, Burma.

the top of the dyke to help 41 Commando clear the village. '48' landed south of the gap, coming ashore in tracked amphibians, LVTs and Weasels. Lt-Col James L. Moulton (later Major General, CB, DSO, OBE) led this Commando which in the next 48 hours with 47 RM Commando, cleared the Germans from batteries along the southern dyke. Their assault was covered at times by air-strikes and fire of medium artillery batteries from across the Scheldt. 41 Commando, meanwhile, with air and naval support cleared the north coast.

4 Commando Brigade later that winter and in the spring of 1945 were in action from time to time in the Allied line in Holland. They carried out a number of raids, including an attack on the strongly defended Kapelsches Veer island in the Maas. Here 400 or so men of 47 Commando

landed on the ice faced dykes in mid-January, but were withdrawn in the face of strong resistance, and the island was later captured by a Canadian brigade over 1,500 strong. We will come back to 1st Commando Brigade, but in Burma and Italy other Marine commandos were in action.[1]

At Kangaw in the Arakan (Burma), 3 Commando Brigade (1, 5, 42(RM) and 44(RM) Commandos) fought off repeated Japanese attacks during early February 1945. Holding vital hill positions despite suicidal Japanese attacks, the problems of re-supply through mangrove swamps and the jungle terrain. In Italy at Comacchio (near Ravenna, Italy) '40' and '43' with 2 Commando Brigade made (with 2 and 9 Army Commandos) an advance of 12km, fighting through entrenched positions across open and flooded ground. In this

This illustration of the beachhead at Kangaw below Hill 170 shows the difficult landing points cleared by RM Commandos on 22–23 January 1945. The Brigade held both the beachhead and Hill 170 despite heavy Japanese counter-attacks during the following week.

Corporal Thomas P. Hunter VC. He was awarded the medal posthumously for deliberately drawing German machine-gun fire while his Section were advancing across open country in northern Italy on 3 April 1945.

action Cpl Tom Hunter, lying exposed on a pile of rubble, drew fire from German heavy machine guns. While he engaged these six or so guns, his Section and the rest of the Troop were able to get forward and under cover. For his self-sacrifice Tom Hunter was awarded the VC.

The 1st Commando Brigade returned to Europe at the time of the Germans' offensive in the Ardennes. In mid-January they were spearheading the British XII Corps' advance into a triangle of well-defended river banks above marshes, where the Maas joins the Roer. In the crisp snow of a clear cold morning, '45' were in the lead near the village of St Joostburg when the forward Troops came under accurate fire from a dyke, the Montforterbeek. Cut off from the Brigade by a German barrage dropped behind '45', they nevertheless reorganised, counterattacked and at times had their own protective barrage a mere 35m from their positions. In these actions L/Cpl Eric Harden RAMC, with complete disregard for his own safety, tended the wounded until he was killed coming back from his third trip in the open within 200m of the enemy. For 'his magnificent example . . . cool courage and determination' he was awarded the VC.

On 23 March (1945) this Commando Brigade made the first of five river crossings. There had only been two weeks to plan and rehearse this operation which was the right prong of 21 Army Group's crossing of the Rhine. The left prong was made by 51 (Highland) Division's four assault battalions in 150 LVT Buffaloes which landed on the north bank at 9 pm that Friday (23 March). Mud slowed the advance of these columns and prevented all their DD (Swimming) Tanks from landing, but nevertheless by dawn they were in the small town of Rees. The 1st Commando Brigade's objective was a much larger area, the city of Wesel (over 20km east of Rees), which would be cut off from the north by the US 17 Airborne Division on Saturday morning. Although the American First Army had crossed the Rhine 140km south-east of here some weeks earlier on 7 March, German resistance was still organised and well dug-in on the north bank opposite the British and Canadian armies.

The assault plan for the Commando Brigade, prepared by XII Corps of which they were now part, was built around a major air attack in which 250 Lancasters, with nearly twice their normal bomb loads, would flatten the city on the night of the assault. All tactical arrangements therefore were contingent on this raid, for without it the Commando Brigade's 'operation must be accounted extremely hazardous' for the force (about 1,200 men) was much smaller than could be expected to hold a well-defended city of that size. Therefore, to keep the Germans uncertain of just how many Commandos had seized it, there would be no vehicles for re-supply passed through their initial bridge-head, which was an inhospitable and unlikely choice of a mud flat, the Grav Insel. From there the Brigade would advance quickly into the built-up area 'on the heels of the RAF'. With the Com-mandos were FOOs and signallers of 1st Mountain Regiment RA, trained to cross difficult country with heavy radio sets. They would direct the fire of the guns which were to provide the Brigade's principal support after the bombing.

On the Friday afternoon, 200 men of an anti-tank regiment helped army engineers and REME fitters to launch 40 storm boats. These were manned by the RM Engineer Troop of the Brigade, and put in the water – each from a 3-ton lorry – on a lagoon 2km west of the crossing point. The Germans were kept occupied at 5.30 pm by a preliminary air raid in which 150 medium bombers hit Wesel 'leaving a great pall of dust over the city'. It was indeed a splendid prelude. From 6 o'clock an almost continuous artillery bombard-ment obscured the German defences, until 46 RM were ready to cross the river in Buffaloes, as operation 'Plunder' got under way.

Six field regiments fired into the opposite (north) bank for ten minutes before H-hour, and with a minute to go the first highsided Buffalo lumbered down the southern bank. The continuous blaze of the field guns' barrage could be seen by the Royal Engineer drivers – lighting the swirling waters of the river, as the swim-ming tracks of the amphibians pushed them slowly across the current at about 100m a minute. Then, after some four minutes, 'B' Troop's LVTs climbed the far bank, but one Buffalo burst into flames; of its 4-man crew and 30 Commandos aboard, only Lt W. J. Allan RM and three Marines were blown free. Despite burns and flesh wounds, they rejoined the rest of the Troop heading for a couple of

buildings and an 88mm gun site 500m behind the bridgehead. 'Y' Troop landed with them and in minutes cleared the trench systems right and left of the land-ing. They took 70 prisoners and 'killed a great number' while 'B' Troop were advancing close to the field artillery barrage now moving forward towards the 88mm site at 100m a minute.

'B' Troop's Sergeant-Major was killed while encouraging the men to keep close to this barrage, which passed over the 88mm's site. A Commando Section then cleared its trench defences, taking 22 prisoners but the gun had been moved away. The Troop were so close to the barrage when they reached the first house that 25-pounder shells were bursting on its roof as they broke in. Two German officers met them at the top of some cellar steps, one was shot but the other ducked back into the cellar. A few 36-grenades and smoke bombs were thrown after him, and the 35 survivors of this onslaught surrendered. 'A' and 'Z' Troops, in the second wave of Buffaloes, were ashore by this time, marching on a compass bearing towards a second building behind the bridgehead. This was shelled in 'a pre-arranged stonk' before 'A' Troop with a section of 'Z' cleared it and the anti-aircraft gun sites nearby, taking 29 prisoners. 'Z' Troop then swung to the left, cleared more weapon pits and estab-lished the outer perimeter of the bridge-head here along the edge of a road.

'The Buffalo ferry (with it's 24 LVTs) was working with clockwork precision' and all five Troops of '46' with the Brigade's advanced (Tactical) HQ were across in 15 minutes. The storm boats carrying 6 (Army) Commando were less successful because their outboard motors proved unreliable. Intense fire from the Manchesters' heavy mortars and machine guns had covered the last moments in the lagoon, and the craft were moving up the southern bank before enemy artillery shelled this launching point. The men of 6 Commando boarded the boats 400m west of the Buffalo ferry, but many boats

Men of 1st Commando
Brigade in the rubble of
Wesel after crossing the
Rhine (see pages 118–24).

were holed by enemy fire. Some sank, one drove its bows under and despite the commandos' life-jackets some were drowned. By 10.30, despite the setbacks, 6 Commando were formed up ready to follow the white tape their lead Section would lay for 4km into Wesel.

The brilliant red flares of RAF Path-finders already lit the city, some falling only 1,000m from the bridgehead, and for the next 15 minutes the whistle of falling bombs and the juddering rumble of their explosion was all that could be heard. The moment they stopped 6 Troop of 6 Commando led off, the Brigade following in single file – a dangerous but effective

and the huge craters, the dust and smoke choking a man as he sweated to keep up with the next ahead.

45 RM and 3 Commando followed 6 Cdo, the only opposition coming from a few riflemen, some with panzerfausts (a crude but effective anti-tank weapon). The Brigade were relying on 'a liberal issue' of these anti-tank weapons captured earlier, to protect themselves against tanks. At the mud flat bridgehead some of the 11 Weasel amphibians (brought over in Buffaloes) helped in evacuating the wounded and by midnight with the dressing-station evacuated to the south bank, the bridgehead had closed down. '46 RM' followed the rest of the Brigade into the city.

'45' now fought their way through streets and gardens to occupy the key northern site, a factory complex which dominated the approaches to the town. Lt Col W. N. Gray DSO, RM was painfully wounded in the advance, but rejoined the advance and by 3 am the Commando was firmly established in the factory. The remainder of the Brigade formed the adjoining tight defence in the north and north-west suburbs. There was no intention with such a comparatively small force, of clearing the town until any threat of counter-attack was over. But from their positions the Brigade were poised to link up with US 17 Airborne Division due to drop north of the city at 10 am that Saturday morning. In the early hours the Weasels 'waddled through the enormous craters' bringing medical stores and radio equipment to Brigade HQ. This was only 'one garden' away from the German HQ of Maj Gen Deutsch, and on discovering this, a patrol of 6 Commando led by the RSM attacked the German staff bunker. The General, bravely resisting capture, was killed by a burst from a Tommy gun. The patrol, joined by the Brigade HQ's Protection Troop, then cleared the bunker, finding many useful maps. However, other Germans outside the city began to react to the attack and from dawn at 5.30 am an SP (self-propelled) gun moved

method of infiltration which they had used in Normandy. The nearly full moon was up, giving a sinister glint to 'the long line of figures filing across the flood plain'. They were checked briefly, while 6 Troop cleared a well-defended 'flak' position, then on into the city. There at midnight they reached the first mounds of rubble

An aerial view of the Wesel factory that was seized and held by 45 RM Commando on 23–24 March 1945. Although there were 23 artillery regiments firing pack-howitzers to 9.2-inch (233mm) heavy guns and 436 aircraft flown in support, the Commando had to rely on their own small arms and mortars for their defence while the American 17 Airborne Division was dropped north of the town.

against '46' and other positions.

'45' were shelled by this gun during the morning, after a cycle patrol had unwarily approached their positions 'and been truly punctured'. Other attacks in Company strength were developing, when at 10 am the first Dakotas and gliders flew in to the north. For the next three hours the Brigade were unable to use artillery support for fear of firing on Allied troops. The Commandos, therefore, had to sit tight, use only their small arms, and fire their anti-tank PIATs angled up in a mortar role having a range of 300m. In the early afternoon two Germany companies could be seen forming up north and east of the factory, but at 1.30 pm – when the 'fire' embargo lifted – the Mountain Regiment's FOO 'turned on the tap' and the enemy and their the SP gun withdrew.

That afternoon (Saturday) the LVT ferry re-opened and by 7 pm the 1st Cheshires, a machine-gun battalion, had joined the Brigade, while patrols made the first contact with the American airborne. The CO of '45', Lt-Col Nicol Gray, was evacuated despite his protests, but his wound needed proper treatment. The few civilians found in the factory's air-raid shelters did not resent the Marines' presence, preferring them to Russians. Other Germans, however, continued the fight even though the first American patrol had reached the factory.

The American Gen Miley, commanding 17 Airborne Division, took the Brigade under his command about 5 am on Sunday. The link-up was complete and '46' had patrols that evening in contact with the 9th US Army to the east. Considering the opposition, Commando casualties were light: '45' had 15 wounded (including the CO) and '46' had 4 killed, 10 wounded and 6 missing. The Brigade had total casualties of 94 (mostly in 6 Commando) but had captured over 850 Germans.

Ten days later, coming under command of the British 6 Airborne Division, they moved north-east in trucks through heavy rain. Congested roads made the 16-hour journey a grim move although only 48km. They then launched a night attack on Osnabruck at 3 am next day, covering the last 6km of their approach in little over an hour. '45' had 3 killed in a burst of Spandau fire, but the town was secured by 9 am, many of the German troops being surprised by the speed of this advance.

45 Commando, commanded since the Colonel's evacuation by Lt-Col Alfred Blake, was detached to reinforce an army battalion with a weak bridgehead across the Weser. Blake intended to capture Lesse, a small town 2.5km southwest of the bridgehead, but the direct approach to it was over flat open ground. Therefore the Commando was working its way south to come into the town from the east, making a wide detour, at first under cover of the bank. They soon met a resolutely held German position. Rifles and sub-machine guns clashed with rockets of panzerfausts and rapid fire of schmeisers in close fighting, during which several young prisoners were taken. They were from 12th SS Training Battalion of Hitler Youth, who showed fanatical courage 'and their sniping was really first class'. Clearly the Germans had reinforced their defences containing the bridgehead, although one of '45's' patrols had reached the railway 500m from the town, Blake was told to consolidate the bridgehead and discontinue the attack on Lesse.

For the next 24 hours, while a bridge was being built, the bridgehead was shelled and its perimeter attacked. 3 (Army) Commando came across in storm boats, but there were too few of these to lift the rest of the Brigade until that night. They then circled to the east of Lesse, surprising the enemy with this night infiltration and took the town by 7 am on 8 April. They had 26 casualties including 4 killed and 13 wounded from '45'.

For this action the Brigade had been under the command of the British 11 Armoured Division, and continued as the Division's spearhead in river crossings. At 8.30 pm on 10 April they crossed the Aller, a difficult operation as the Germans

Royal Marines paraded on the deck of the German heavy cruiser *Prinz Eugen* in May 1945.

were able to defend wooded ground north-east of this river. In the battle which developed next morning three German battalions were unable to break the defence of the bridgehead, for by this time commandos knew that to stay alive they needed a good slit trench, one young officer digging five that morning. Nevertheless, the Brigade had 125 casualties. They moved on a week later, and stormed across the Elbe on 29 April against 20mm fire from a bluff near the landing point; in 45 minutes after the first landing at 2 am, the whole Brigade had landed. '46' then led the advance, seizing high ground 1.5km from the bridgehead and 'behind' (north of) Lauenburg. Meanwhile German aeroplanes attacked sappers building a bridge for the Division's armour. Yet in spite of this, the armour crossed the Elbe and by 30 April the town had been secured by army battalions.

August in southern Malaya. The war against Japan seemed likely, however, to be a long campaign and plans were afoot to bring the total strength of Commandos in south-east Asia to 4,300. In this force was the Small Operations Group (over 200 'swimmers' who since early in 1945 had mounted reconnaissance and decoy raids). This Group co-ordinated all small-scale amphibious raids in this theatre, by army and navy parties and the Royal Marines of Detachment 385.

'385' had been formed in 1944 from 100 selected volunteers, mostly from the MNBDOs, whose special training included not only long-distance swimming and canoe techniques. A number of men were taught astral navigation, others learnt to select sites for forward airstrips, some learnt to use limpet mines as RMBPD had done at Bordeaux, and another group was given additional training in demolitions, before the first raid was mounted in February 1945. In this, No. 2 Troop with three Sections each of 9 or 10 men, was to raid three villages on the Burmese coast 320km south of Akyab. On the night of 22 February they landed with varying fortunes.

No. 1 section landed successfully, the surf boat being hidden in mangrove swamps, before the party moved across the beach and along a jungle path. They were nearing the village, 2km from the boat, when shots rang out from the landing point. On going back they were fired on by two light machine guns, an awkward moment for they did not know if the enemy had captured their boat.

Maj Duncan Johnston, who had led Force 'Viper', now took the raiders back across the sands towards a 50m wide channel. Cpl Smith disappeared about this time, probably drowned as they took cover under the steep bank of the river. They wore Mae West inflatable lifejackets and the swim across this channel did not seem far – except for those who forgot to blow-up their jackets in the excitement. Coming to the north bank, they were again fired on for the night was light with

This was the Commandos' last battle in northwest Europe. In Italy 2 Commando Brigade's 40 RM and 43 RM with 2 and 9 Army Commandos had continued their battles in the flooded Po valley, where the Germans surrendered on 3 May, and five days later all German organised resistance ceased.

In India 3 Commando Brigade, after their successful actions in Kangaw, were training for the landings to be made that

a full moon and cloudless sky. Maj Johnston was killed but the men decided that in a couple of spirited dashes they could reach the boat 200m away. This they did, pushing her while up to their necks in water, but every movement drew more machine gun fire. They fired a red Verey light, the signal for covering fire from the motor launch, and bursts of 40mm Bofors' rounds 'whizzed over our heads'. The Verey flare, being damp, had fallen too close for comfort but as it guttered out the men clambered into the boat, for the Japanese had stopped firing. Maj Johnston's body was hauled aboard, and kneeling to paddle the men rowed away from the beach. Their troubles were not over, for it took 20 minutes to get some little way out. Nevertheless, they covered the 2km to the waiting motor launch by paddling, 'encouraged' by occasional bursts of enemy fire. They had taken nearly $4\frac{1}{2}$ hours from leaving to rejoining the motor launch at 1.30 am.

No. 2 Section landing in similar fashion, found two Burmese hiding in a bush who the interpreter questioned. He learnt that Japanese patrols were looking for them; they therefore withdrew back to the motor launch. No. 3 Section landed at the most northerly of the three villages, where they were engaged in a fire fight but successfully withdrew back to the motor launch.

Early in March several parties were

Men of Detachment 385 launch an inflatable craft from a Catalina flying-boat in preparation for a raid somewhere in south-east Asia. Raids were made for beach reconnaissance and to deceive the Japanese on likely invasion points on the Malayan coast and the islands of south-east Asia.

landed on Phuket island off the west coast of Siam just north of the Malaysian peninsular. They came 'unstuck' because there were too many raiders involved, and during their first 48 hours ashore they attracted the attention of local fishermen. Although individual raiders survived for a week or more in the jungle, eventually all were killed or captured. Maj John Maxwell RM and C/Sgt E. C. Smith of '385' were taken to Singapore, where they were imprisoned with survivors of the clandestine Section Z. This Section had attempted to raid shipping in Singapore but the junk carrying their canoes had

Japanese staff officers report to Lt-Col G. B. Grant RM on the quayside at Penang during its reoccupation by the British in August 1945. Royal Marines from HMS *Nelson* and other ships of the Far Eastern Fleet (including Landing Ships Infantry one of which can be seen in the background with her LCAs on davits) were landed to secure the island.

been caught by Japanese naval patrols. Among these canoeists was Maj R. M. Ingleton RM who the previous year served in the Armoured Support Group. On 5 July these prisoners, with great bravery, said 'good-bye to each other, cheerful to the end', before the firing squad finally extinguished 'the valorous spirit of these men' in the words of their executioners. Six weeks later on 14 August 1945 the Japanese surrendered bringing World War II to an end.

There had been plans to employ six RM Beach Groups – the original purpose of RM Brigades diverted to Europe in the Spring of 1945 – as well as Commandos and Fleet Marines in the Pacific. But in the aftermath of World War II, the Corps was given the sole responsibility for Commando operations and the Army's Commandos were disbanded. Over 63,000 'HO' Marines were demobilised – see Note 4 of Chapter 4 – with a well conceived approach to their training for civilian jobs during the run-down period. There were happy and some sad memories for all of them, and none appear to have left the Corps without great respect for its traditions, a sense of its family and lasting affection in the retrospect of old age.

Chapter 7

Withdrawal from the Empire

3 Commando Brigade RM, as the only peacetime Commando Brigade is known, was serving in Hong Kong when the last Army Commandos left to rejoin their regiments in 1946. Their duties would follow a broad pattern of actions and deployments covering the final stages of British involvement in her Far East and Mediterranean territories.[1] After nearly two years in Hong Kong where they had formed the garrison, helped to prevent smuggling, raided opium dens and carried out other internal security (IS) duties, the Brigade moved to Malta. It would serve overseas from 1944 to 1971, 27 years without a break, before returning to the UK. In the Mediterranean elements of the Brigade served in the Canal Zone, and in 1948 covered the final withdrawal from Palestine. The next year they were back in the Far East and in May 1950 first deployed in Malaya.

Brig Campbell Hardy DSO, who had led the Brigade at Kangaw in 1945, was again in command (later he would be Commandant General). His three Commandos, 40, 42 and 45 RM, would spend the next two years in jungle patrols, re-settling local squatters and developing that co-operation between civilian police and the military which is so essential in these situations of near civil war. Their first area – Perak State – was about the size of Wales, with tin mines and plantations to the west bordering swamps, thick jungle to the east rising to the mountains along the Thai (Siam) border. Here a man could spend a cold night in ambush and within the month find he was in the steamy swamps of the western jungle. Indeed, dogged persistence, hard work

and some luck is needed to catch terrorists; one officer, leading a patrol in 1950, later learnt from captured documents that he had passed within metres of the enemy. They, thinking this small party to be merely an advance guard, did not attack but instead let them go by. Such are the fortunes in this type of warfare.

Good training, an eye for ground, and firm leadership enabled the Brigade to keep down battle casualties to 30, while accounting for over 200 hard-core terrorists. In Korea, where 41 (Independent) Commando fought a very different war against Chinese forces in 1951, losses were much greater. That November '41' was attached to the US 1 Marine Division on the Chosin Plateau, and in fighting through with a relief column to reach the Division's base, '41' lost 70 men of 200 who set out. Their action that day (28 November) further fostered the long standing regard between the Corps and the US Marines. They came out with the Division ten days later in a fighting retreat, and for their actions were awarded a United States Presidential citation.

A year later, the Brigade was back in Malta, and would serve in Egypt and Cyprus and train in North Africa during the next nine years. In October 1953 they carried out the first combined amphibious exercise with the US Marine Corps, since World War II; and during this period they first developed their skills in landing from helicopters. During the conflicts between Greek and Turkish Cypriots, when the pro-Greek EOKA terrorists were hidden away in the Troodos mountains, cordon-and-search operations would need to be quickly mounted.

Left: 41 (Independent) Commando RM on the snow-covered plateau of Chosin, Korea in December 1950. In action under the command of 1 USMC (United States Marine Corps), they were supplied by air drops after being surrounded by Chinese forces and fought their way to the Divisional forward base. For this and other actions they were awarded the Presidential Citation.

Below: Amtracs, tracked amphibians, launched on 7 April 1951 from USS *Fort Marion* carry men of 41 (I) Commando for a raid near Songjin over 250km behind North Korean lines.

Right: Commandos landed from USS *Fort Marion,* having blasted holes with 'Beehive' charges, prepare demolition charges of 18kg to destroy a section of railway-line running from Songjin to the Manchurian border on 7 April 1951 during the Korean War.

Below: Iban trackers, who worked with RM Commandos in Malaya in the early 1950s. They could find trails even across hard ground and located bandits' routes which the commandos would then ambush.

The Marines were also in action in 1956 during the Suez Crisis. '40' and '42' landed in the van of the assault on Port Said in November 1956, and '45' made the first British helicopter unit landing into a battle area. The Commandos landing by LVT and LCA were ashore and had established an initial beachhead into which '45' were brought by Whirlwinds and the tiny Sycamore helicopters. (The latter each carried three Commandos, the outside two with their legs over the side of the chopper with each man holding a 106-mm shell.) The Brigade Commander, Brig Rex Madoc who had been in the Crete rearguard, had his HQ near the beach with his men in a 3km radius across hostile streets. British paratroops dropped the previous day held the airfield west of the town and French paras held the east bank of the canal, before an uneasy 'and somewhat one-sided' truce was arranged that night. And next day, in the face of political pressures the British and French governments allowed no further advance towards Suez. Most of the Brigade were then withdrawn after a week.

Further tours in Cyprus, training in Malta, and North Africa as part of NATO's southern flank force, followed. The concept of the helicopter Commando Ship was also developing at this time, for the landings of '45' at Port Said had shown this to be feasible. It was also much faster than using LCAs or LVTs as we will see in the next chapter.

The Commandos had 10 fatal casualties during their 1950s tours of Cyprus before returning to the Far East in 1961. Meanwhile 45 Commando had begun what would become a $7\frac{1}{2}$-year tour in Aden. A Marine normally serving there for a year, would – by what is known as 'trickle drafting' – be replaced, so that while the Unit was overseas for many years, individuals were not. The first Commandos to land in Aden in April 1960 were sent to join the British garrison in this colony and its much larger Protectorate, an area half the size of France but with only 800,000 people. Here on the Yemeni border at Dhala or in the vast mountain wastes of the Radfan, the Commando was engaged

in a series of counter-terrorist actions from 1964 until the final withdrawal at the end of November 1967. Long before then the Brigade – based in Singapore from April 1961 – was deployed in Borneo

Above: Z Troop of 45 Commando patrol Yerolakkos in the spring of 1956. Here in Cyprus the Royal Marines first made use of specially trained dogs to work with the anti-terrorist patrols.

Left: A Whirlwind helicopter lands men of 45 Commando near the statue of de Lesseps, Port Said on the morning of 6 November 1956 during the Suez Invasion. Each Whirlwind carried 5–7 men while the smaller Sycamore carried 3.

The routes taken by 40, 42 and 45 Commando of 3 Brigade when they seized Port Said on 6 November 1956 in the opening phase of the Suez landing.

during the Indonesians' confrontation of the newly formed Federation of Malaysian States which included three territories in north Borneo.

The first serious threat to the authority of the Sultan of Brunei came in December 1962, when rebels occupied a number of towns including his capital and in neighbouring Sarawak (which surrounds Bru-

nei) and Sabah to the east. On Monday 11 December 'L' Company of 42 Commando was flown in to Brunei (modern Bandar Seri Begawa) which Gurkha troops of the British Army had secured for the Sultan. Capt J. J. Moore (later Major General OBE, MC and bar) found the town still had many houses on stilts over the river, while the jungle swamps near the

coast could only be crossed by boat. Therefore, the river gave the only practical approach to reach British hostages who were being held by the rebels at Limbang in neighbouring Sarawak, for HMS *Albion* with her helicopters was steaming from Mombassa and several days away. Yet next day the hostages were, it was reported, to be killed.

Two RN minesweepers were in Brunei and their crews fitted out a couple of river barges which that night sailed for Limbang. Capt Moore, expecting the hostages to be in the police station, planned to land there about first light, knowing that quick action would be essential as at least 150 armed rebels were in the town. Despite engine breakdowns and narrow water-

Royal Marine Commando

The first major British force landed into a battle area by helicopter, as men of 45 Commando are brought into a landing zone in Port Said, 6 November 1956.

Royal Marine Commando

When Iraqi forces threatened Kuwait, 42 Commando was landed by helicopters from the Commando Ship HMS *Bulwark* and 45 Commando were flown in by RAF transports from Aden. This bren gunner of 42 Commando holds a position on the low hills of the desert during July 1961, the hottest time of the year in one of the hottest parts of the world.

An RM commando sentry in Aden in 1967 where 42 and 45 Commandos covered the final withdrawal after the British handed over security responsibilities to the National Liberation Front (NLF).

ways, the barges were just 275m from the police station not long after the street lights were switched off. The Company's Intelligence Sergeant's loudhailer call for the rebels to lay down their arms was met by machine gun, rifle and shot-gun blasts. Over 300 rebels joined in the fire fight, but the Commandos' Vickers machine guns kept the initiative. The first barge forced its bow ashore near the police station, two Marines being killed before the craft hit the bank. Lt 'Paddy' Davis was wounded but Sgt Bickford led two Sections ashore, and in minutes they had cleared the police station.

Meanwhile, the cox'n of the second craft had been hit, and it drifted past the landing point but fortunately was driven ashore near the hospital 150m further up-stream. Here they found the principal hostages unharmed, although one attempt had been made to shoot them. That night rebels were killed inside the Marines' perimeter but next day the town was secured.

During the next $3\frac{1}{2}$ years both '40' and

45 Commando served for nearly three years in the arid mountain country of the Radfan, south Arabia. Here Section Commander Corporal D. Dorling, his GPMG gunner and three other marines of 7 troop, Z Company patrol a high rock-strewn plateau.

'42' Commando would serve in Borneo, along with several thousand British army troops including Gurkhas. By 1964 each Commando had built up an expertise in this difficult type of warfare, with disease – including an invariably fatal fever carried by lice on river rats – a greater danger than enemy action. That July, for example, 40 Commando did their first tour on the north-east of the island – previously they had been in Sarawak – but here at Tawau a small town of less than 4,500 people on the east coast of Sabah, the East Brigade had their HQ. The Commanding Officer was a Malaysian and the Brigade Major British, but in order to avoid any political difficulties the more adventurous operations were not carried out under the Brigade commanders' orders, since on occasions these might take the Commandos across the border, an almost unavoidable action in, for example, the maze of shallow waterways behind this coast. Here the Tawau Assault Group, men of 40 Commando, patrolled in dorys and native boats from their bases deep in the maze of waterways, always at risk of ambush from the overhanging jungle or poisonous yellow-and-black snakes falling into a boat. They found little, but by this date Indonesian regular forces from southern Borneo crossed into Sabah, and the boat crews found some Indonesian kit.

The need to contain these regular troops led to Commandos raiding into the Indonesian 'half' of Sebatik island. Marine

A patrol of 42 Commando with local forces move through the jungle in Borneo in November 1963.

Royal Marine Commando

L Company of 42 Commando storm ashore against heavy fire to rescue British hostages held by 350 rebels in the village of Limbang, Sarawak on 12 December 1956. Five Marines were killed and six men wounded including a naval Petty Officer.

Commandos distribute clothing to villagers on one of the many occasions when they helped the local people, for (in the words of an RM Assault Engineer) they 'engineered much and assaulted nobody' when distributing food and building bridges and community schools in Borneo.

canoeists also made raids and in 1963 two men swam ashore to reconnoitre an Indonesian observation post (OP). This OP on the south-east shore of Sebatik Island faced Nanukan Island on which Indonesian Marines had a base. A raiding party of Marines from 40 Commando later made an attack on this OP. Three Gemini inflatables were launched from *Bob Sawyer* (a small motor cruiser) north-west of Sebatik and were paddled down the coast on the night of 8 December 1963, one staying near the border with a support party and their GPMG. The assault Gemini's continued their 9km approach to a sandy strip some 70m west of the OP and an *atap* hut nearby; led by Lt R. A. M.

Seeger these 15 Marines included a GPMG, a close-quarter assault group with SMGs and two scouts with an improvised night vision device of electric torch fixed to each SLR. The scouts job was to stand-off or cut-off – depending how the action went – the men in the OP.

'Ram' Seeger had no sooner beached his leading boat than it came under in-accurate fire. He shouted 'spread out left and assault forward' as he moved towards the OP, Sgt Costley and Mne Allan bringing the GPMG into action along the water's edge to the right. As he ran forward, the Lieutenant stumbled but was up again, the flicker of the Indonesians' camp fire guiding him and the GPMG

team who moved along the shore waist-deep in the sea. In the starglow Ram Seeger crossed several open patches of ground to suddenly see the hut loom up. His shout of 'Grenades' made the GMPG team duck under the water holding their guns over their heads, and the Lieutenant's two M26 grenades burst in the doorway. He followed in firing his SMG so that a more or less continuous stream of 9-mm 'preceded him to the front door'.

The narrow beach with thick jungle behind it had slowed the assault group but they soon joined Seeger, to fan out across the beach. There was no time to search the hut as they had been ordered not to get involved in any prolonged action, but three bodies could be seen in the firelight. The Marines' withdrawal was quick; back to their landing point pushing off in the inflatables before opening up the outboards' throttles. Mortar fire had begun to fall near the OP and small arms fire whistled overhead but no one was hit, except Ram Seeger who had found early in the action that 'a bullet had gone through the flesh of his elbow'. He was awarded the MC, Sgt Costley and Cpl Tomlin (who had led the close-quarters group) were both mentioned in despatches. Further raids were carried out to nip any danger in the bud before it flowered across the border. Other attempts at containing invading companies of Indonesians

The many waterways of north Borneo were patrolled by commandos, sometimes using 2-man canoes, during the $3\frac{1}{2}$ years of their tours at the time of the Indonesian confrontation.

A typical fort from which
commandos patrolled the
Borneo jungles.

were less successful. The 1960s equivalent
of a floating battery with one or two 5.5-in
(140-mm) medium artillery guns sank. Or
at least only got off some 50 rounds before
it was too waterlogged to fire more.

Across the bay from Tawau was the
centre for log exports, Kalakaban, with its
pools filled with teak logs ready to be
rafted out to ships. The workforce, however, were indistinguishable from Indonesians for most commandos. The lumber
company's British manager made the
Commando officers welcome, and '40's'
accommodation was improved with new
huts. They were relieved by '42', who had
been carried away perhaps by reports of
comfortable living for they brought the
trappings of their officers' mess. Un-
fortunately – certainly by no connivance
of '40' – the trailer carrying these was
dropped into the harbour while being
offloaded.

More crucial was the damage the damp
and rain – the mornings were often
beautifully fine but by the afternoon it

was pouring – could do to an SLR (Self
Loading Rifle) or a machine gun. The
ammunition for the GPMG (General Purpose Machine Gun) could also become
mildewed or worse, but the men realised
the importance of keeping this unboxed
ammunition clean and kept their rifles
well oiled.

'40's' next tour in Borneo was more
lively when they returned in July 1965 to
the north-west coast of Sarawak with
their HQ at Serian. The Commandos – reorganised from five Troops to four and
later three companies – were along the
Indonesian border in hilly country covered almost entirely with jungle. Here, for
example, 'B' Company had a fire base at
Pang Amo. The local people were paid to
build these 'forts', which at Pang Amo had
the leaf-roofed *bashas* with open sides.
From beneath these ran a 'bolt-hole' to the
fire trench, with its corrugated-iron revet-
ment, linked to the sandbagged HQ dug-
out and the 105-mm pack howitzer position in the centre of the fort. Water was

A 105mm gun of 145 Battery, 29 Commando Light Regiment, (later 29 Commando Regiment), RA prepares for action in support of 42 Commando in Borneo, 1965.

pumped up to storage tanks and after filtering could be drunk. All this equipment had to be flown in, RAF Belvedere helicopters bringing large loads of corrugated iron and other supplies. Food and ammunition was parachuted in from RAF Argosys and New Zealand Air Force Bristol freighters, usually in five or six 1-ton loads dropped outside the perimeter for fear of 'leg pulling should they hit the *basha*'.

The fort was on a pimple topped hill, in an ideal position to dominate the area, even if stores from an air drop had to be hauled up the hill. There was no way to make the defence inconspicuous and therefore the Company relied on a bold show of force to deter attacks, their mortars and GPMGs ever ready to fire on any hostile approach. Although paths joined the villages (*kampongs*) there was only a difficult march from 'B' Company's fort to 'A' Company's position some 5km to the south-east, but not to 'C' Company nearly 10km away 'as the helicopter flies'.

Chopper was the only practical form of communication, and the small RM helicopters attached to '42' carried company commanders, emergency supplies and occasionally sick natives to the nearest clinic. Although Troops – now the equivalent of an Army platoon – were on occasion flown piece-meal so to speak, by the small Sycamore helicopter, the larger Wessex Fleet Air Arm choppers were used to ferry them around. This was necessary to reinforce forts from time to time, for among the steady 'foot traffic' of locals carrying pepper on its way to the coast, were Indonesian raiding parties.

To intercept these, patrols would be sent out (typically a Troop of Commandos) in 'long' ambush routine. In this the men slept at night beside their ambush position with GPMGs manned to cover the killing ground, their four gunners changing watch every hour or so. Some 50m beyond the ambush and further down the track towards an enemy's likely approach was a Claymore mine which could be triggered by remote control. There were occasional accidents, when, for example, a night fisherman ignored the curfew. At other times, by sleeping by their ambush points, men could be alerted and ready and the moment the GPMG fired the men silently rolled into position. Any other method meant staying awake five nights on the trot after marching all day, or moving from 'bivvies' to the ambush at an alarm, neither of which was likely to produce the quick reactions needed in night ambushes.

Late in August it was decided to make a 2-Troop recce of the border south of Pang Amo, and on Monday 28 August they moved south. Here the Recce Troop with their radios were left on high ground to relay messages from the patrol back the 7km to the Fort. At dawn next day they moved a kilometre west and then 400m south, distances to be measured in time not metres for the hills were covered in jungle and rise here to between 700 and 1,000m. That night they bivouacked, having cut their way round bamboo thickets, for going through these was both time-consuming and noisy. Each man carried two water bottles but the bulk of even their dehydrated rations took up room in their packs. (Men on an 8-day patrol have been known to get by on 5 days' rations). In their harbour 'bivvies' with two to a tent-sheet *basha*, most men slept in a piece of black parachute silk (from supply drops), which was warm but rolled into a small bundle as did the inflatable pillows some men used. They only carried one mess tin and plastic spoons to avoid telltale jangles when moving. For although they had seen no tracks nor sign of locals, they knew from reports of Border Scouts that the Indonesians had a camp not far away – 2km by air from the Recce Troop's position. On Wednesday the main patrol moved southwest in the camp's direction to form a forward base in mid-afternoon.

Two patrols – each of about 10 men – went out and in a couple of hours reported a lot of bamboo to the south-west and a suitable ambush position on the track to the east. At first light next morning one Troop occupied the ambush position and two Sections of the second, 17 men, probed south for a better view of Peripin village and its *bashas*. The Company HQ with the Troops remained in the forward base, where the Forward Observation Officer (FOO) was also in contact with the 105-mm at the fort, but the patrol was nearing the gun's maximum range. As the two Sections moved cautiously along the edge of a clearing, they could not see the *bashas* north of the village, used by Indonesian soldiers. A slow but steady advance was bringing them nearer to a sight of these, however, after six hours careful stalking. The leading Commando scout was nearing the bank of a stream, when he saw a soldier looking at him from the roof of one *basha* 30m away.

Firing broke out, two soldiers on the roof were hit, and light machine gun and rifle fire came from both *bashas*. Grenades – fired from rifle dischargers – were sent into the roof and under the enemy's huts before their firing slackened, although grenades still fell within 3m of the Marines. A heavier Indonesian gun now fired on a fixed line (at a pre-determined position of aim) by chance between the Sections, and the Commando's 105-mm's fire was called down on the area. After a little over 10 minutes, the Lieutenant leading the Sections withdrew them and only inaccurate mortar fire followed their retreat. Meanwhile the Troop from the ambush was brought forward to cover this withdrawal and about 3 pm fired down into the huts at long range. Plunging fire from SLR, GPMG, light mortars and M26 Grenades was brought down on the *bashas*, there were now seen to be four, and accurate fire continued from the 105-mm.

Sections reoccupied the ambush position but the withdrawal was not followed up, and picking up their packs as they passed through the forward base, they marched back to the hill position of the Recce Troop. This Troop remained to cover the return to the fort where the

Sections arrived next morning.

One man had been badly wounded but he could not be airlifted out that night as there was no suitable site for a chopper to land, and in the pitch dark of a wet night he had been carried to the fort. There the Company continued its routine. There were letters to the OC requesting pregnant wives be airlifted to Serian clinic, requests to join the Sarawak Rangers, requests to hunt monkeys near rice crops and a hundred similar village matters to be cleared up. But the Marines had always to be on their guard for strangers, so nobody for the most private reasons strayed out of sight of the GPMG gunners on watch from the fort.

Some months later, leaving decoy patrols in the fort area, some 40 men of 'B' Company again made a wide sweep to recce Peripin which they had been told was unoccupied. But to the OC's surprise, when he approached the apparently deserted huts, he found he was looking at two Indonesian soldiers, one cleaning his boots and the other eating a meal. Two others had passed the OC out of his sight in 'dead' ground, before they walked within 15m of the GPMG. They were shot, tumbling base-over-apex back down towards the stream. At this moment the OC and the forward Troop's commander were nearly shot by their own Marines as they raced back to get behind their cover. The second Troop, advancing to cover those already forward, was also fired on from Peripin at this time, a Marine moving forward being hit. He was mortally wounded when shots exploded ammunition he was carrying as he lay in the open. With the Troop in their new cover, the GPMGs fired again but the enemy's mortars this time were firing accurately, nevertheless a Marine went out to the injured man and brought him under the cover of a low rise in the ground.

The Company had orders not to become engaged in a prolonged fire fight and so withdrew. The 105-mm in the fort 9km to the rear again gave them accurate covering fire, its fall of shot being directed 'in

25-yard steps' by a Troop commander. The Troops fell back, 'pepper potting' – that is: moving in dispersed groups one Section moving, one giving covering fire – until they were out of range of the enemy *bashas*. Although exact numbers of the enemy could not be checked, these huts housed the Peripin garrison which was 25–30 strong, its Indonesian soldiers smartly turned out, as the shoe-cleaning suggests. Had their skill at arms been as good, many more Marines would have been casualties than the one Corporal killed and 2 Marines wounded.

42 Commando also had their share of patrolling in Borneo, when they might drop in pairs from the trees, with 6km to go to an assembly point. By this date the Marines had perfected the art of roping down from a chopper to treetops 70m above the primary jungle's floor. This height may seem a long 'drop' but by abseiling with clips to hold the rope pressed over your thigh, the fall was at a controlled speed to some extent depending on the weight a man carried. Although those dehydrated rations – enough for 10 men for 24 hours in a pack of 20cm by 15 by 30 – were light, if eaten as solids they seized up a man's innards. The men had a choice in the rations they carried as they did in matters of dress and gear within broad limits. The locally made (by the Commando's cooks) rations were marginally the most popular, with lightweight rations the next preference to army-type 'compo'. The cooks handled – or more hygienically dealt with – over 70,000 eggs, 700 chickens, 6 tons of meat in about four months. The forward supply NCO climbing a 1,000m into the hills to deliver rations by porters when bad weather prevented air drops.

On patrol, keeping off tracks to avoid mines, men had to be good 'navigators' and if ever you have tried to follow a compass bearing through a wood you will realise how difficult this is. Not only were the men able to move quietly but they did not use their cookers nor wash with scented soap for the smell of these could waft a kilometre or two from camp.

As 'L' and 'M' Companies prepared for a fighting reconnaissance south of the border village of Biawak in mid-May 1966, they were to mount a classical operation. The companies made a long approach march over a couple of days, harbouring at night. On the third day they moved close to an Indonesian stronghold, and continued their advance after dark – a most difficult and dangerous movement through jungle but they reached the enemy's *bashas* without being detected. Nor were they discovered when Claymore mines were laid from long bamboo poles onto the roof of the enemy's huts. The enemy did not react until – to their shock – these were detonated, each flinging 700 steel balls through the *basha* roofs. As a fire fight then developed many Indonesians were killed by the Marines' GPMGs and Armalites. Their only casualty was Capt Ian Clark who died from his wounds.

Although the Marines had used SLR rifles since 1959, during their tours in Borneo '42' used Armalites, which are lighter (at 2.8kg) than the SLR (4.3kg) but fire a high velocity bullet though without the stopping power of the heavier rifle. By one report, nevertheless, the Armalite proved 'to be a good substitute for a sub-machine gun', although after the operations in the Borneo the SLR remained the Corps' principal rifle, as it had been for '45' during their time in Aden. There this Commando had spent over three years up-country in the Radfan – as mentioned earlier – and by June 1967 were almost as familiar with its arid mountain ranges as were the tribesmen.

Their first operation there in May 1964 was a night infiltration – shades of Normandy and Wesel – a long file of men stealing into the mountains to have their rock-built sangers established on 'Coca-Cola' hilltop just before dawn. A few days later they moved farther into hostile territory, but a company of the 3rd Parachute Battalion, under '45's' command were caught in daylight by accurate fire before they reached comparative safety on a hill top. In the subsequent battle a para lieutenant was killed and a number of men wounded, but by the fifth day of the operation the tribesmen had left the area of Danaba. This major stronghold was in the north-west corner of some 10,000 square kilometres of rugged terrain which British and Federal Forces came to dominate but never subdue. '45', alternating with Para and other British Battalions, made many patrols, laid ambushes and travelled long distances despite the heat. In one period of eight weeks, they also made 305 major night patrols, which were particularly disconcerting for the tribesmen who did not normally fight at night.

In daylight the Commandos worked closely with RAF Hunters, which Forward Air Control (FAC) officers could direct onto targets from the ground or from the FAC's helicopter. However, showers of lethal empty 30-mm cartridges from these fighters caused at least one serious casualty in '45'; in part because Commandos had not worn steel-helmets in action since the summer of 1944, preferring the 'freedom' of a green beret or the 'floppy' hat all British troops wore in the tropics. The significance of the green beret, feared by Axis forces in World War II for the aggressive patrols and attacks of the Commandos, had by the 1960s become internationally recognised. For the British it was – and is – the hallmark of an independent, self-disciplined Marine, who alone if needs be, fights his way to his objective against any odds.

These characteristics were needed in plenty during the Corps' last days in Aden, as the British force were preparing to finally withdraw; and the feuding factions in Aden fought each other. They also vied with each other in their attacks on the British, so 'X' Company knew what to expect when called to support army units in Crater. This bed of an extinct volcano, with its high black walls cutting off the sea breeze, formed a natural oven in which a warren of shabby streets housed Arabs, Indians, Pakistanis, Jews,

Somalis and a few sophisticated terrorists. Only two roadways lead over the lip of the rock walls, and these are in the Main Pass to the north-west of the town. Above them on the west side are old Turkish battlements which were held by Arab nationalists, who also were firing down the country (north) side of the pass on 21 June 1967. The previous day two patrols of Argylls and Royal Northumberland Fusiliers (RNF) had been massacred in the town, and the British had decided to withdraw for 'the aim was pacification and that meant the least possible force'.

'X' Company came under command of the RNF on the afternoon of 21 June and moved to regain Main Pass. The Queen's Dragoon Guards' armoured Saladin cars and RNF machine guns covered their advance, as men of the Company's Support Group – without their mortars – led up the left (east) side towards the rock rim. They had to cover the last 40m exposed to fire from the battlements, but nevertheless got GPMGs to the east of the valley looking – and firing – across into the battlements. Their fire was so intense, that guns and crews changed over after each had fired two belts ('liners'), for GPMGs overheat if fired continuously. Under cover of this fire the rest of the Company picked their way up this side of the pass. As dusk fell, a Section made their way across to the battlements but the Arabs had gone. Perhaps, as an eyewitness suggests, 'it was the clanking of the aluminium signal ladder the Section carried, that had frightened the Arabs away!' Be that as it may, in the next few days the Marines were fired on from time to time, but only replied with rifles for the Saladin's 76-mm would have killed more civilians than terrorists. One persistent sniper, however, firing from a house on the town (southern) slope of the Pass had to be silence by a single round from the Marines' anti-tank Carl Gustav.

The Royal Marines unlike the Army, had retained the skill of snipers and in the next two weeks they proved invaluable. High in their hides among the rock face's caves, they made roofs in the town untenable in daylight for those who would fire at the Company holding the pass. These snipers knew where each shot would strike – 15 hits from 24 rounds being the overall score – with an effective use of few rounds. While each of '45's' companies did a 4-day spell at a road block on the Pass, through which up to 6,000 people a day were checked, not counting the goats. During this time down in the town, the NLF and FLOSY fought for control of the streets. Then, on 3 July, the Argylls moved back into the town. (Snipers did not always escape from counter fire, however, and on at least two occasions wounded men spent an uncomfortable number of hours waiting for dark. A good 'hide' was not to be given away by hasty evacuation before night, even had it been safe to move in daylight.)

By September '45' were deployed in Ma'alla, a town of *Kutcha* huts, where FLOSY had a large following. Here the technique of using well fortified observation posts (OPs) was perfected, for the four men in each sandbagged emplacement had to assess any sudden movement seen by one of them through his binoculars. Was it a grenade thrower? A disturbance needing a ground patrol to check-out what was happening? Or an incident to be immediately reported to the Company's Command Post? Only the men in the OP could decide. Fire the GPMG at innocent folk and there would be an 'inquest', fail to report a minor flare-up between Arabs and in minutes the Company might have a riot on their hands. Each of 16 OPs was on the Company radio 'net' and intelligence officers, who for some years had been working with the local police, kept the observers informed on what – and who – to look for.

The Commando's radio net was perhaps more complex than most at that time. In addition to the OPs and mobile patrols on the 'net', up to 36 out-stations might be manned. An intelligence officer's unmarked car, the armoured $\frac{1}{2}$-ton truck of the Recce Troop, or other special patrols,

Sioux Bell 47G light helicopters of the RM Commando Flights fly over Singapore with an Army Air Corps Scout helicopter. These Flights later formed 3 Commando Brigade Air Squadron.

could then report incidents to Company HQs in their Command Posts, while Commando HQ monitored these reports. In this way the reserve Troop of a Company might be quickly brought to an incident and any escalation covered by redeployments the Colonel made to nip trouble in the bud.

Lt-Col J. I. H. Owen (later Major General, OBE) commanded '45' at the time of the final withdrawal. They had been joined by '42' in October, brought in by the commando ship HMS *Albion*. Col Owen had the 400-year-old Turkish harbour fortifications sandbagged and reinforced, for this so-called 'Owen Line' would be used in the final phase of the withdrawal; meanwhile detailed plans for every eventuality were made.

HMS *Albion* supplied the Commandos ashore, her workshops and sick-bay meeting the needs of the men in what was becoming a beachhead on Steamer Point. By this time in mid-November army units had completed their withdrawal and nearly 700 crates of RM heavy equipment were shipped out and 300 were airlifted. RM lieutenants and Naval 'schoolies' – Intelligence Officers when on operations – took over interrogations of suspects, a job 'normally the responsibility of higher echelons'. So far as they could, Marines

also prevented pilfering; but apocryphal or not there are some amusing tales of the greedy being thwarted. Well! If you buy two heavy duty refrigerators on a quay in these conditions for next to nothing, you should hardly be surprised if the dock gate sentries will not let you take them out.

On the night 24–25 November the line of OPs overlooking Ma'alla were evacuated and '45' manned the 'Owen' line. At 1.25 am (25 November) '45' set off for Khormaksar airport, guarded now by '42'. Col Owen's Land Rover with its escort passed into the airfield perimeter 25 seconds late. 'Not bad' the *Globe and Laurel* commented 'after 139 years'. Four days later '45' were flown out while '42' held the line of defence posts across the Point to prevent mortars getting in range of the airfield.

Next day, the defences were handed over to the South Arabian Army and '42' were lifted out by helicopter to *Albion*. One of her LCA's bowman was probably the last British serviceman to leave, when he slipped the bow rope from the quay as the craft brought out the last British official to leave Aden. Royal Marines would be in new deployments in the 1970s but the Brigade did not leave Singapore until 1971 on the final withdrawal of the British presence east of Suez.

Chapter 8

Commando Ships and Europe's Northern Flank: The Corps' Modern Roles

During the years of withdrawal from the British Empire, the commando ships HMS *Albion* and HMS *Bulwark* had operated in the Mediterranean or the South China Sea in support of Commandos ashore. Their Fleet Air Arm Squadrons of helicopters, a few of these aircraft flown by Marines but mostly Royal Navy crews, were able not only to land Commandos but also to supply them for months on end while fighting ashore. 848 Squadron, for example, in 1967 flying 18 Westland Wessex Mark V helicopters off *Albion* in her third commission as a commando ship, having spent most of the two previous commissions off Borneo in 1964–66.

Royal Marines also provided landing craft crews and beach control parties from their Assault Squadrons (see Appendix 2). These served aboard both the commando ships (called Landing Platforms Helicopter, LPHs) and the LPDs. There are two of the latter : HMS *Fearless* (colloquial 'Fearnought') and *Intrepid*, which since 1966 and 1967 respectively had provided a means for landing the army's tanks by LCM. These Landing Platform Docks are equipped with all the communications gear of radios, visual display units and other so-called 'systems' of a complete command HQ ship, and are able, when required, to control the landing of a Brigade or even larger formations of troops with their supporting aircraft and missile ships.

Life in an LPH was much the same as at sea in other fleet aircraft carriers, although the embarked commandos slept in three-tiered bunks which folded away to give some living space in the mess deck. In the LPDs, the 'Barracks' as Marines' mess-decks are still called, are relatively spacious and being forward in the ship are close to the canteen and the ship's laundry. Aft in an LPD is the covered over dock, into which the cox'n of an LCM – larger than the World War II craft – has to manouvre his craft. No easy matter with the ship flooded down and her stern gate open, steaming slowly for steerage way while taking in or launching her four LCM. She also carries LCVPs, descendants of the LCAs, slung on davits 12m from the water. On the flight deck over the dock are facilities, known as 'Spots', for five helicopters.

From *Intrepid* in November 1970, helicopters flew to the relief of Bengalis caught in a cyclone and its tidal waves. As they flew over the devastated estuary of the Ganges, only tops of coconut trees swayed above the vast expanse of brown water, for the water level was some 8m above the normal height. Near the higher ground away from the shorelines, 'the stench of death was unforgettable' even when flying 30m above the waters. Piles of bodies, washed into pathetic groups, lay not far from the survivors. They were clustered in groups around red flags, the sign that food and fresh water were needed. Yet to land too close to these men – most of the women and young children had been swept away by the flood – was to court disaster, as the refugees had sometimes literally plucked helicopters from the air, the weight of humanity crashing the aircraft onto the ground before it could land properly. As each chopper touched down some way from the red flags, nevertheless, in seconds it was besieged by frenzied Bengalis. They tore open sacks of rice and

Royal Marine Commando

Admiral of the Fleet the Earl Mountbatten of Burma, Life Colonel Commandant of the Corps 1965–79, seen here in his Royal Marine uniform. His ancestor the Prince of Hesse Darmstadt commanded the Marines at Gibraltar, the start of the family's long association with the Royal Marines.

A Mark 9 LCM from HMS *Intrepid* carries ashore the Beach Armoured Recovery Vehicle (BARV) used to tow out vehicles bogged down in mud and refloat craft stranded on the beaches.

Opposite above: Raiding is a traditional role of the Royal Marines which they have continued in the 1980s. Here E Company return to their parent ship after a night 'raid' in the Mediterranean. This is just one of the specialist skills of the Royal Marines that made them an essential and highly valued arm of the British task force in the Falkland Islands crisis, 1982.

Opposite below: RM commandos improvise a river crossing during exercises in July 1980 in the New Hebrides where they were on peace-keeping duties.

ate it raw, although Commandos acting as aircrew handlers tried to keep some form of order. Many helicopter crews flew up to 16 hours a day during the first days of this relief operation, for the ships had to lie nearly 50km from the inshore islands as the floods had silted up the bay.

These were long voyages for the LCM crews, each with their Colour Sergeant coxswains, from *Intrepid* and the stores ships to the off-loading points up muddy rivers. The landing craft brought ashore vehicles, fork-lift trucks and up to 70 tons of food each trip, while 150 men of 3 Commando Brigade set up an advanced relief centre at Patuakhali 68km south of Dacca. Army and RAF units were also deployed to distribute the 20 tons of baby food, feeding bottles and medical supplies, as well as bulk foods brought in from the ships. *Intrepid*, using her Headquarters ship communications, co-ordinated the aircraft and other movements.

On several occasions when help has been needed in 'times of trouble' the RM Raiding Squadrons have been sent to

peoples' aid. However, their main military purpose is to put ashore raiding parties, not unlike those described earlier landing on the coast of Japanese occupied Malaya, but in the 1970s and '80s the 'kit' is much more sophisticated. Speeding along at 40 knots or more in their fast little power boats, the raiders skim across the sea – or bounce on occasions in rough water – to hurtle their craft up a beach. The noise of their outboards would awaken a dead sentry, but one suspects they have ways of stealing ashore. However they land, these men are experts in demolition, in ways to cause mayhem behind an enemy's lines and snatching vital intelligence from under his nose. The more peaceful uses bring the stranded family from flooded areas or the would-be cliff climber from his unhappy choice of picnic spot.

The Corps has played its part with other British services in bringing help to communities in trouble through the years. The earthquake victims of Iierossos,

A Hovercraft lands the Michigan '175' of an RM Beach Party; this tractor lays beach roadway as it moves forward, enabling wheeled vehicles to cross shingle.

Greece in 1932 saw the Royal Navy and Royal Marines as 'Angels' in their town's time of trouble. In Borneo, RM assault engineers turned their hand literally to bridging the gap between peoples: 'they engineered much and assaulted nobody' in the words of one of them. Among their list of military engineering works are 'dammed river (for children's swimming pool), built bear pen, strengthened huts, fitted gas geysers, and contributed to Hearts and Minds'. Such work left a legacy of goodwill after the withdrawal from the Empire. But some of these operations can be as risky as – if not more so than – actions in a battle.

On the morning of 18 May 1972 a terrorist phone call threatened an explosion aboard a ship at sea 'by 9 pm tonight'. The authorities took this seriously and two Royal Marine commandos, Lt Richard Clifford and Cpl Tom Jones were called from Poole to the RAF station at Lyneham (Wilts). There they met for the first time Capt R. Williams RAOC, an expert in bomb disposal and a Staff Sergeant of the Special Air Service. The sergeant was a parachutist as were the two Marines, but Capt Williams had only

made a few jumps and took time out on his way to Lyneham to refresh his scant training in parachute drills. There was no time to waste in getting aboard the aircraft, as there was a sense of urgency.

Their Hercules aircraft took off about 4.15 pm for what would be a 4½-hour flight; their RAF 'dispatcher', gave a hand with the stowing of their equipment and the five men had time to talk over their plans. They discovered that the Captain had never made a drop into water, so they went over the drills – when to unbuckle the harness, how to keep clear of the canopy floating down on the parachutist-swimmer, how to stay afloat (in this case some half hour or more perhaps) until a boat picked him up. The loads were re-shuffled so that Cpl Jones and the Sergeant would carry the bulk in two heavy loads each over 45kg and Richard Clifford would have the third of about 18kg on a line with a breaking strain of 680kg. They had been told as they took off that the ship was the *Queen Elizabeth II* carrying nearly 2,000 passengers and crew in mid-Atlantic. Many lives were at stake and risks might have to be taken to reach them.

The first to drop would be the NCOs carrying the heavy loads but as experienced parachutists they were 'able to cope'. Richard Clifford and Capt Williams, would be in the second drop with the Marine taking care of the inexperienced jumper. As they flew near the ship, they found an overcast sky with cloud at about 150m, the wind gusting to 20 knots. It would be a difficult landing coming down across the choppy sea at the speed of a city bus, the canopy dragging you through the water too fast to unbuckle the harness if you had not got the drill right. The overcast sky gave added problems, since you need some 300m of fall should you have to use a reserve chute. They could not fly at this height and still see the intended dropping zone; therefore they agreed to jump at 240m.

The RAF pilot of the Hercules made several passes over the QEII and radio contact was established. She would put out one motor cutter downwind of the ship, where her bulk gave some shelter from the worst of the seas. Then the pilot surged up to 240m, forgetting perhaps that this acceleration would make his passengers and their loads weightless. The plane made a further pass over the ship and out went the NCOs, who made a successful descent and freed themselves from the parachute harnesses, their heavy loads being held by 3m of line from each man's waist.

Ron Williams was now sick and Richard Clifford had to reassure him; on the third pass after the first stick went out, the RM Lieutenant, with a growing sense of urgency, pushed his charge and they dropped through the door nearly together. Not the best way to start a descent but there was now less than two hours to the threatened time of the explosion and the QEII's suspect cargo would take time to defuse. As they went through the 'door' Richard Clifford's line to his load was broken and Capt Williams' reserve chute was ripped off. But they both splashed down safely and the Marine swam to his charge, keeping him afloat for 10 minutes

or more until the cutter arrived. About 8.40 pm they were aboard the liner and immediately began searching the suspect cargo. No bombs were found, but it had been a risky operation for which both RM Commandos and the rest of the team received the Queen's Commendation for Bravery. When a similar incident occurred on the Oriana seven years later, Richard Clifford again led the team but the jump was cancelled by the ship's captain when the plane was overhead.

Richard Clifford later made three single-handed crossings of the Atlantic, once being capsized and needing all his commando resourcefulness, determination and guts to complete the crossing with a jury compass and considerable damage. The commandos enjoy other equally venturesome sports including sky diving, long-distance canoeing and climbing. In Greenland on one such expedition in the winter of 1967 the 8-man adventure team of soldiers and Marines explored the region, mapped it and made scientific studies. They were several hundred kilometres from the nearest road, and climbing previous unexplored peaks. Lt Terry Thompson RM was moving along a ridge, before rocks suddenly gave way and although he only fell 3m he broke his leg and dislocated an ankle. He was given first aid, then lowered 500m down a steep snow gully and carried across rough tundra country 8km to the base camp. From there, his leg still in improvised splints, he was taken by a local boat to hospital. Meanwhile the expedition successfully climbed 'Wedding Cake' mountain of 1,300m in the Sukkertoppen area of the coast. 'Adventure training' as such expeditions are sometimes called, involve many such incidents, and have taken place in Greenland, in the Antarctic, in South America, Switzerland and the Himalayas.

In 1980 the RN and RM Mountaineering Club sent an expedition led by Capt David V. Nicholls RM to North India. There in nine weeks they climbed the 2,000m north-west face of Phabrang (6,200m) which had not been conquered before.

One of 42 Commando's fast Rigid Raiders intercepts a junk in autumn 1979 in a search for illegal immigrants attempting to enter Hong Kong.

They had spent many months in carefully preparing for this climb, all had some experience and four were from the Mountain and Arctic Warfare Cadre RM or had served in this specialist unit. Yet there are risks ever present at these heights in snow conditions, and during an exploratory climb on Tent Peak (6,010m), Maj J. M. Patchett (Gurkha Rifles) was caught by a large rockfall which 'suddenly descended the gulley' he was climbing. Badly injured, he had to be carried 500m back down this gulley, an arduous 3-hour climb. The Major was then made comfortable but it took two days to reach the nearest long range radio and call help from the Indian Air Force. The teams coming off Phrabrang were to meet with a fatal accident, for in glisading down a familiar snowslope he had crossed the previous day, Chief Petty Officer R. G. Thomas RN lost control of his slide. Although an experienced mountaineer, he could not prevent himself going over the edge of a 500m cliff. He was extremely badly injured and died the next day.

The Commandos' service in the 1970s and early '80s had taken them to Ireland. Although too recent in time for any historical perspective, these deployments have their dangers. Nevertheless Commandos have proved their steadiness in the face of provocations in difficult situations. These they also find further afield, in Hong Kong, for example, helping to keep track of illegal immigrants. This work distressed the men of '42' for many were women and children, but had Marines not rescued numbers of them from their precarious rafts they would have drowned. Half a world away, in Belize (Central America), the New Hebrides (Pacific) and Rhodesia/Zimbabwe, deployments have in recent years taken Marine Commandos on peacekeeping missions. 41 Commando have also made several tours with United Nations Forces in Cyprus.

Royal Marines still serve in ships, but no longer does every capital ship carry Marines. The small detachments of the 1980s, all commando-trained, serve in selected smaller ships or may be embarked in the aircraft carriers when necessary.

Men of 40 Commando on fire-fighting duties in Glasgow in 1979.

Marines of 40 Commando take a well-earned respite while on an exercise.

A Carl Gustav 84mm RCL, a light anti-tank weapon, is fired by Mne George Lee on an exercise in 1978. In April 1982 a large Argentinian force seized the island of South Georgia in the Falkland Islands invasion. Before being overwhelmed, the garrison of 22 Marines destroyed an assault helicopter and used a Carl Gustav to cripple a missile corvette in the first ever action between a warship and a modern anti-tank weapon.

Major (acting Lt-Col) David Drysdale RM (right) talks to officials at assembly point 'Mike' during the Commonwealth Monitoring Force's deployment in Rhodesia-Zimbabwe in 1980. He is wearing the Monitoring Force's arm-band.

Above: A patrol of 41 Commando in riot gear on the streets of Belfast during peace-keeping duties in 1970.

Left: A four-man Section from 40 Commando in a shooting incident in New Lodge, Belfast in 1971.

Opposite above: Commando recruits land from a Westland Wessex helicopter while on a training course near Lympstone.

Opposite below left: RM commandos fire a Wombat, one of their principal anti-tank weapons in the 1970s. This 120-mm recoilless gun fired a small missile up to an effective range of 1000 metres and was ranged onto the target by the 0.5 inch (12.7mm) spotting rifle mounted on the line of the gun. The Wombat began to be replaced by the Milan from 1981.

Opposite below right: A commando in NBC (Nuclear, Biological and Chemical warfare) clothing, with his SLR (Self Loading Rifle) camouflaged by white tape, leads a patrol during a deployment in Norway.

Above: Two occasions for ceremony. (*Above left*) The Royal Marines Band of the Commander-in-Chief Naval Home Command beat Retreat at Broadlands, then the home of Lord Mountbatten, on 5 August 1974. (*Above right*) The Queen's and the Regimental Colours of 41 Commando are marched through the Jubilee Gate of Deal Barracks in May 1981 upon the Commando's disbandment.

Left: A commando GPMG gunner and a rifleman take up firing positions during a jungle exercise. Royal Marines are trained to serve anywhere from the polar regions to the tropics.

Above: Realism is a feature of RM commando training as in this contest of unarmed combat.

Right: A team from 42 Commando Group RM play a local team in the New Hebrides, July 1980.

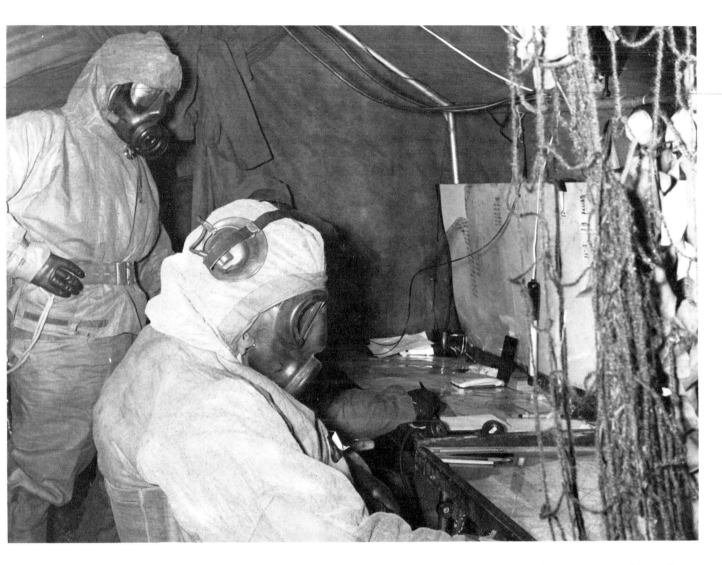

RM commando signallers in NBC (Nuclear, Biological and Chemical) warfare suits during an exercise in 1981.

The conditions – bunk beds, dining 'halls', and cafeteria messing – are very different from Nelson's day or indeed those of World War II. But detachments are still sent away in boats, albeit Gemini inflatables or the fast 'Atlantic' cutters. Lowered by powered winches, with quick release falls, these boats' powerful engines can drive them at a lively speed across rough water. You may bounce around more than oarsmen in a pulling boat, but you get where you are going a lot quicker.

Modern warships carry helicopters principally for anti-submarine work, but a frigate's Wasp can lift several Marines a few at a time to an emergency. This may be part of an exercise on some oil platform or the investigation of apparently unfriendly strangers visiting an uninhabited island. Ashore the Brigade have their Air Squadron with Gazelles and Scout helicopters, nippy choppers able to fit a GPMG for air-borne fire support on occasions, carry a Commando CO for his recce or spot the fall of shot from the Royal Artillery's 105-mm guns of 29 Commando Regiment, formerly Commando Light Regiment. Other Army forces serve in the Commando Logistic Regiment and 59 Independent Commando Squadron Royal Engineers.

The artillery, transport and engineer units are attached to individual Commandos from time to time forming a Commando Group which carries 'quite a punch' in the view of American staffs, for it can fight as an independent force. Two of these groups ('45' and '42') with Brigade Headquarters, deploy each January in North Norway. There have been

Men of 3 Commando Brigade on an exercise. All men of the Brigade with its 42 and 45 Commandos, the Commando Logistic Regiment, attached Royal Artillery gunners and Royal Engineers of 59 Independent Squadron are arctic trained. (*Above*) A commando parachutes into 'action'. (*Above centre*) A 'stick' of commandos wait to be airlifted to new positions. (*Below centre*) A 105-mm light gun of 29 Commando Regiment RA is prepared for action. In the background is a Volvo BV202E oversnow tracked vehicle. (*Below far right*) Commandos with a Wombat on a stripped down Snowtrac. (*Above far right*) Men of 3 Commando Brigade on a ski patrol.

Marine Commandos training with Norwegians since World War II, but only in recent years has the Brigade operated there in force. A good deal of experience and special skills are needed to survive in the remote mountains of this region north of the Arctic Circle; to fight there on NATO's northern flank will definitely require the whole gamut of commando qualities, for on a typical company patrol men may ski 25km a day carrying 30kg loads, sleeping at night in 2-man snow holes. These become almost pleasantly warm, melting any loose snow the careless may have brought in on their clothes, while spreading polystyrene sleeping mats on which sleeping bags are insulated from the snow floor.

A ski patrol can fire while on the move; more effective is the use of ski-sticks to provide a bi-pod 'stand' for aiming an SLR. This may be done when there is the threat of nuclear, biological or chemical warfare (NBC), with all the impedimenta – not to say, 'clobber' – of respirator (gas mask) and heavy protective suits with their carbon-absorbent granules in the fabric. These suits may be as essential to survival as the snow-hole or Arctic equipment, for the Russians may use such nerve gasses as *Soman* or other chemical agents sprayed from aircraft, tanks or by multi-barrelled rocket launchers 18 of which can put down 720 rounds in 20 seconds. For men without respirators such vapours or droplets can cause the nervous system to collapse – first your vision is blurred, you cannot co-ordinate your movements and then your breathing is stifled – in one to ten minutes. Even drops on the skin or clothing can have this effect in half an hour, unless you are wearing protective clothing.

Therefore, as the Commando companies deploy to protect their anti-tank weapons, the key to mastery of any aggressor in modern war, they may well have to contend with all the difficulties of fighting in their NBC suits. They will be supplied by load-carrying choppers, the 3-ton trucks of the 1980s, provided these can fly for in North Norway snowstorms can create 'white-outs' when ground and sky are indistinguishable. Then the LCVP and LCM, with their protective covering against the weather and no doubt against chemical vapours, will come again into their own. Just as the Independent Companies fighting in Norway in 1940 found fishing boats an ideal means of supply transport, so in the 1980s landing craft could serve this purpose. Operating as they can from their own forward base, the Mark 9 LCM can land 70 tonnes of stores or armoured vehicles on beach-roadway laid by the Assault Squadron of which the craft are part.

Will Derby, unused to his new type of

Royal Naval medical teams have served with RM Commandos since 1942. Here a casualty is prepared for evacuation by nurses and Royal Marines from the Medical Squadron.

flintlock musket in 1664, would find warfare in the 1980s to be more than a 'push-button' affair. Helicopters may fly in firing anti-tank weapons, armour may move at high speed over rough country, and hydrofoil ships cruise at over 50 knots, but Will Derby would recognise the steady hand and cool courage of the commando in his firing position. After all the weaponry has been deployed, and Commando HQs know a trick or three about this from their experience of controlling LPD operations, it is the commando on the ground who will fight the battles. The traditions of tenacity in defence of Gibraltar, of those who stormed Belle Isle's cliffs, welded to that of the Rangers leading the defence and the RM battalions attacking them in the redoubt on Bunker Hill, will help to sustain him, perhaps. He may know of the RMLI privates' isolation at Inkerman, of the grim realities of losses in Flanders and Normandy, he will probably have heard of commando operations in south-east Asia and the arid Radfan. What is certain is that he will add his own page to these glorious traditions of the Royal Marines Commandos, written in blood so that men remain free.

Survival practice the hard way. Corporal Bruce Quinn with 45 Commando takes a dip at −15° Centigrade while on exercise in Norway.

Overleaf: Commandos climb a steep slope during an exercise in north Norway.

Appendix 1

Abbreviations

AE Assault Engineer; **AFV** Armoured Fighting Vehicle; **AG** Adjutant General; **AVRE** Armoured Vehicle Royal Engineers; **Bde** Brigade; **Brig** Brigadier; **Bn** Battalion; **bty** Battery; **Capt** Captain; **Cdo** Commando Unit; **cdo** (individual) commando; **CG** Commandant General; **C-in-C** Commander-in-Chief; **CO** Commanding Officer; **Col** Colonel; **coy** Company; **Cpl** Corporal; **CSM** Company Sergeant Major; **D-day** First day of an operation (obsolete); **DAMS** Defensively Armed Merchant Ship (WWI); **DEMS** Defensively Equipped Merchant Ship (WWII); **DZ** Dropping Zone; **FAA** Fleet Air Arm; **FAC** Forward Air Control; **FOB** Forward Officer Bombardment; **FOO** Forward Observation Officer; **Gen** General; **GHQ** General Headquarters; **GOC** General Officer Commanding; **GPMG** General Purpose Machine Gun; **H-hour** Time of landing; **IS** Internal Security; **LC** Landing Craft; **LCA** Landing Craft Assault; **LCF** Landing Craft Flak; **LCG(L)** Landing Craft Gun (Large); **LCI(S)** Landing Craft Infantry (Small); **LCM** Landing Craft Mechanised; **LCOCU** Landing Craft Obstruction Clearance Unit;

LCP Landing Craft Personnel; **LCS** Landing Craft Support; **LCVP** Landing Craft Vehicle and Personnel; **Lt** Lieutenant; **Lt-Cdr** Lieutenant Commander; **M and AW** Mountain and Arctic Warfare; **Maj** Major; **MG** Machine Gun; **MGRM** Major General Royal Marines; **MLC** Motor Landing Craft; **MN** Merchant Navy; **MNBDO** Mobile Naval Base Defence Organisation; **MOA** Marine Officers Attendant; **MOD** Ministry of Defence; **NATO** North Atlantic Treaty Organisation; **NBC** Nuclear, Biological and Chemical (warfare); **NCO** Non-commissioned Officer; **OC** Officer Commanding; **OCRM** Officer Commanding Royal Marines; **OP** Observation Post; **Ops** Operations; **ORs** Other Ranks (Enlisted Men); **Pte** Private; **QF** Quick Firing; **QMS** Quartermaster Sergeant; **Q-ship** Decoy merchant ship with hidden guns; **RA** Royal Artillery; **RE** Royal Engineers; **Regt** Regiment; **REME** Royal Electrical And Mechanical Engineers; **RFA** Royal Fleet Auxiliary; **RL** Recce Leader (obsolete); **RM** Royal Marine; **RMA** Royal Marine Artillery; **RMLI** Royal Marine Light Infantry; **RSM** Regimental Sergeant Major; **SBS** Special Boat Section or Squadron; **SC** Swimmer Canoeist; **Sgt** Sergeant; **S/L** Searchlight; **SLR** Self Loading Rifle; **SMG** Sub Machine Gun; **SOE** Special Operations Executive; **Sqn** Squadron; **Tac HQ** Tactical Headquarters; **T/S** Transmitting Station; **TSM** Troop Sergeant Major; **USMC** United States Marine Corps.

Appendix 2

Organisation of Marine and Royal Marines Forces

The Duke of York and Albany's Maritime Regiment of Foot 1664–85. Formed on 28 Oct 1664, The Regiment's colonel, lt-colonel and major also commanded companies (coys) as did the three captains. The regiment initially had 6 companies with 200 privates but after various changes there were 14 coys of 60 privates by 1668. The Regiment was known as The Lord High Admiral's Regt or The Admiral's Regt, but when the Duke of York, the future James II, resigned from this office because as a Catholic he was barred from such appointments in 1673, he kept The Regt as His Royal Highness's Regt or the Duke's Regt.

A battalion of 8 additional coys was formed in 1678 sometimes known as Sir Oliver Lyttleton's Regt, but was disbanded by April 1679 when the possibility of a war with France had passed.

Prince George, Hereditary Prince of Denmark's Regiment 1685–89. When the Duke of York succeeded to the throne, his son-in-law Prince George took the Maritime Regt under his care. The officers received a new commission on 11 Feb 1685, in what was now called Prince George's Regt or the Prince's Regt. A grenadier coy was added to make 13 coys in all by the early summer. (A previous coy had been trained as grenadiers after service in Virginia in 1678). The effective strength of the Regiment declined in the following years; and 15 days after William III and Mary came to the throne, the Regiment was disbanded on 28 Feb 1689.

Marine Regiments of Foot 1689–99. 2 Regiments formed June 1689 with the intention of one serving at sea while the other garrisonned naval ports. These 1st and 2nd Marine Regts were known by their colonel's names but were a third below establishment by Dec 1696. As from 31 July 1698 the 1st Mnes absorbed the 2nd Mnes, although before they were disbanded a 'new' 2nd Mnes and the 3rd and 4th Mne Regts were briefly raised, their colonels from July 1698 all being officers who had previously commanded line regiments. The COs were: 1st Mnes – the Earl of Torrington and later the Earl of Danby, and from 31 July 1698 Col Thomas Brudenall; 2nd Mnes – the Earl of Pembroke, from 31 July 1698 Col William Seymour; 3rd Mnes – Col Edward Dutton Colt; and 4th Mnes – Col Henry Mordaunt.

Marine Regiments of Foot 1702–13. 6 Marine Regt and 6 line regiments for sea service were raised on 1 June 1702. Each Mne Regt had 12 coys and was known by its colonel's name. At sea and ashore they were 'paid in like manner to land forces' but their cost was met by the Admiralty, and they received extra pay for work in the dockyards as labourers, etc. The COs were: 1st Mnes – Col Henry Holt; 2nd Mnes – Col George Villiers, Col Luttrell, Col Willis; 3rd Mnes – Col Edward Fox, Col Bor; 4th Mnes – Col Henry Mordaunt, Col Viscount Shannon (see below); 5th Mnes – Col Thomas Saunderson; and 6th Mnes – Viscount Shannon.

The 5th and 6th Mnes were disbanded in 1708 and for some years the 4th Mnes were replaced by Brig General Seymour's Queen's Regt but these returned to the line in 1711, when the 4th Regt was probably reformed to be disbanded in 1713 when the 1st, 2nd and 3rd Mnes became line regiments as the 30th, 31st and 32nd.

Marine Regiments of 1739–48. 1st to 6th Mne Regt raised in Dec 1739 with cadres from Foot Guards and Col Edward Wolfe as Adjutant General. Each Regiment had 9 line companies and a grenadier company, all based on 70 privates, with apparently a drafting margin. The Regiments' total strength was raised by 2040 men in 1740 and a further four Regiments raised in 1741, the corresponding (Army) line regimental numbers being 44th to 53rd by this date. Their total establishment of 10,000 compares with the Army's strength of 85,600 by one report, and they became 'incorporate with the line', before being disbanded in 1748, by which date the mixing of different Marine Regts in ships' detachments had made their administration impractical.

The Corps from 1755 to 1816. A Marine Mutiny Act of 1755 established a Corps of independent Marine Companies, the number of which was fixed by order-in-council from time to time. In April 50 coys were assembling at Chatham (12), Portsmouth (20) and Plymouth (18), with some men from the former Marine Regts. Each port's companies were commanded by a lt-colonel with a major as second-in-command and officers commissioned in specific coys. The Admiralty issued orders to each group of coys or Grand Division, but the senior officer from Portsmouth informally represented The Corps in London.

All ranks were embarked according to a sea duty roster but there were some inequalities over the time different men had to serve at sea. There were also sinecure appointments from which two Admirals and three naval captains were paid as generals and colonels respectively, in the Marine Forces. These 'Blue Colonelcies' paid £800 a year in 1760 and were not abolished until 1837.

Companies of RM Artillery (RMA) were formed at each Division in Aug 1804, these coys were paid Royal Artillery rates and later an RMA headquarters was opened at Chatham. The following year the Woolwich Division was opened with 30 coys bringing the Corps' establishment to 143. The RMA coys by 1813 had an increased proportion of NCOs for in addition to the larger number of small detachments in 'bombs' etc, the RMA trained other troops in artillery.

The Corps from 1816 to 1913. After the Napoleonic Wars the Corps was finally reduced to 80 coys, and officers were attached to Divisions not commissioned in specific coys, with the RMA coys all in Chatham commanded by a Major Commandant. The Colonel Commandants at the four Divisions had their staff initially reduced as was that of the Commandant in Town, 6 Colonel Second Commandants retiring on full pay, but most were later recalled. In 1831-36 an Army Officer as Inspector General of Royal Marines, replaced the Deputy Adjutant General (DAG), but in 1832 a Marine General was again appointed DAG with an RM officer as his deputy. Responsibility for the Corps' finances passed that year (1832) to the Accountant General of the Navy and the post of Paymaster was abolished.

Promotion was extremely slow, some captains being retired in 1834 to give promotion to lieutenants of 26 to 29 years standing. The RMA was reduced to a nucleus of 2 coys as the navy took over all gunnery establishments, although RMA and RMLI officers had been employed as gunnery officers since 1829 and all ranks in the Corps were involved in naval gunnery. With the introduction of steam gun boats and similar vessels, more RMA gunners were needed and the 3 RMA coys raised to 14 by 1859 when they formed a separate Division. The infantry companies were designated RM Light Infantry in 1855 and the two arms continued until amalgamation in 1923, but the Woolwich Division was disbanded in 1869. The training Depot at Deal was opened in 1861 and some recruit training continued there until the 1970s.

In 1877 RMLI other ranks (enlisted men) were first able to gain the same gunnery specialist qualifications as seamen. For the first time in 1879 Marines serving on land became subject to the Army Acts.

From 1903 the Corps became responsible not only for its own bands but for all naval music with the formation of the RM Band Service which as the RM School of Music continues in the 1980s.

The Corps in World War I 1914-18. The principle of Port Divisions providing detachments for ships at sea continued throughout the war, and they also provided men for the DAMS, Howitzer Bde and other units. Replacements for casualties in the RM Bns were trained at Blandford (Dorset) in a camp built to train the Naval Division. From Jan 1915 the RM instructors were under Naval Command, until June 1916 when – although they remained at Blandford – they trained Reserve Bns under the administration of the War Office. For a detailed description of the Corps' organisation in WWI see *Britain's Sea Soldiers: a record of the Royal Marines during the War 1914-1918* by General Sir H E Blumberg KCB.

The Corps 1919-39. After World War I the reduction of Britain's armed forces led to an amalgamation of the RMA and the RMLI. The Adjutant General (AG) with his staff in the RM Office in Whitehall continued to have overall responsibility for the Corps with staffs at each Division, but as the AG was responsible to the Second Sea Lord who in turn was mainly responsible for finding men to man ships, the Corps had little influence in high-level planning at the Admiralty. Bns for overseas service were found from time-to-time from the drafting margin of Mnes serving ashore in spells between 'commissions'. The Reserve consisted almost entirely of regulars who had gone to pension.

This organisation had many drawbacks, perhaps the principal of which was the limited opportunities for senior officers to control major formations of troops. Nor was the Corps allowed to raise a Strike Force to seize an advanced base for the Navy. They were, however, asked to develop methods of landing heavy guns and equipment to protect such a base. From these trials came the Mobile Naval Base Defence Organisation and considerable know-how for a relatively few – but influential – number of the Corps.

The Corps in World War II 1939-45. The Corps continued to provide ships' detachments from the Divisions and by 1940 had begun to train volunteers to provide the manpower for a Strike Force, their initial training was undertaken at a new National Service camp Lympstone, and other camps were opened. At first there was only one Bde with 3 battalions but it was expanded to an amphibious Division with eventually two brigade groups; but it was not until after Aug 1943, when the Amphibious Division and the MNBDOs were broken up, that the Corps became widely involved in operations.

The Commandos – '40' formed in Feb 1942, '41' (Oct 42), '42', '43', '44', '45', '46', '47' (all provided by Bns from the Division) in Aug 1943, '48' from MNBDO II's 7th Bn in Mar 1944 – were brigaded with Army Cdos, the HQ of the Division providing personnel for the Cdo Group's HQ. At the same time in 1943 the Corps took on a new commitment in manning the navy's assault craft. These flotillas were under naval command much as the guns' crews continued to be in capital ships, while the Army's Cdo Bdes with their Group HQ were under the Army's operational command. The Adjutant General, briefly as GOC RM, before the title was changed to Commandant General (CG), continued to administer and direct the training of recruits. Although the Corps continued to be a department in the 2nd Sea Lord's jurisdiction, it had many ties of unofficial but great moment in government circles: with Churchill strongly in favour of the Corps and Lord Mountbatten as Chief of Combined Operations the man who did most to ensure its future in Commandos.

By the end of the War the versatility of the detachments and units serving in the Corps – from 14-inch naval guns' crew to canoe raiding parties, from armoured amphibians' crews to communications specialists – was wider than it had ever been. For details of these units see *Royal Marines 1919–1980* by J D Ladd.

The Corps from 1946. In 1946 the traditional organisation by Port Divisions, which had provided detachments for ships based on Chatham, Portsmouth or Plymouth, was no longer required. The Corps, therefore, reorganised in two stages, to concentrate commando Group HQ in the Plymouth area, Training Group with landing craft crews at Portsmouth (and later at Poole) and the ships' detachments with pay and records based on Chatham until this HQ closed in 1950. From that year the ships' detachments, greatly reduced in numbers since World War II, have been part of the Portsmouth Group, Poole.

The Cdo Group provide a Brigade HQ with 2 or 3 Cdos depending on the operational requirements in the Near and Far East, for this 3 Cdo Bde RM remained abroad first in Hong Kong (to May 1947), then in the Mediterranean and Egypt until May 1950 when it returned to the Far East. They returned to the Mediterranean from March 1952 before their final tour of 10 years in the Far East, returning to the UK in 1971. This Bde at first under RN command, later came under the Army's operational command for most of its time abroad. While Commandos based in the UK were detached to Army commands as required for operations, taking their turn with Army Bns as Spearhead Bn in the UK strategic reserve. After 1 April 1964 the Commandant General and his department in London became integrated with the naval staff, CG taking his place as the head of a department and a senior commander of naval forces under the Vice-Chief of the Naval Staff.

In the 1980s the Corps is organised to provide an Arctic Warfare Bde with two Commandos, an independent cdo, a large coy (Comacchio Coy) for the defence of naval and other installations, a number of 10-man detachments for service on frigates etc, Assault Sqns manning landing craft and with beach control parties, Raiding Sqns with high-speed craft and a number of other specialised units. The RM Band Service provides bands for a number of Naval Commands and for ships, including the Royal Yacht.

For a detailed study in changes in the organisation over these years see *Royal Marines 1919–1980* by J D Ladd.

Notes

CHAPTER ONE

1 Examples of actions and deployments of Maritime Regts 1664–1755.

2nd Anglo-Dutch War 1665–67. 1664: Adml's Regt at Southampton, 250 men at sea, Nov. *1665:* Battle of Lowestoft, 13 June; summer in port garrisons. *1666:* Four Day Fight, 11–14 June; Battle of North Foreland, 4–5 Aug. *1667:* with West Indies sqn, May; in Kent defences, June; in Harwich defences, July.

3rd Anglo-Dutch War 1667–74. 1672: at capture of Dutch ships before war declared, Mar; Battle of Solebay, 27 May. *1673:* 1st and 2nd sea Battles of Schooneveldt, 28 May and 3 June; Battle of Texel, 11 Aug.

No Maritime Regts 1688–89.

War of the Grand Alliance 1688–97. 1690: Battle of Beachy Head, 29 June; coys in Cork, Ireland, Sept. *1692:* Battle of Harfleur, 19–25 May; coys in Jamaica, summer. *1693:* in a force at St Malo, Nov. *1694:* summer with ships blockading French trade. *1695:* with Mediterranean sqn.

No Maritime Regt 1699–1701.

War of the Spanish Succession 1702–13. 1702: in a force seizing treasure in Vigo, Spain, 12 Oct. *1704:* landed with Dutch and took Gibraltar, July, besieged there for 9 months; took heavy casualties at sea off Gibraltar, 13 Aug. *1705:* in a force taking Barcelona, Aug; besieged there until May 1706; at 11 different ship actions mainly against French privateers. *1706:* formed garrison of Cartagena, Spain, 1 June; in capture of Ostend, Belgium, 25 June; in a force capturing Alicante, Spain, 28–29 July; besieged there until withdrawn, Apr 1708; formed first Majorca garrison, Sept. *1707:* in a force landed to destroy defences near Nice, France, 29 June; in a force besieging Toulon, France, 15 June–6 Aug. *1708:* in action on Sardinia, *Aug–Sept;* in a force seizing Annoplois Royal, Nova Scotia, 24 Sept.

No Maritime Regts 1748–54.

2 Colonial Marine Regts 1740–42. These 2 Regts of 'Gooch's Marines' were commanded by the American colonial Col Gooch. All the officers were colonials except for one Marine officer appointed as adviser to each of the 36 coys. The total strength of 4,000 had to be made up from 'indentured servants, impoverished Irishmen and criminals' and by the spring of 1741 sickness, desertions and transfers to the navy had reduced the regts to 43 officers and 1,388 men. 500 more men were raised in America and from escaped slaves before the regts were in action at Cartagena in modern Colombia, where they lost most of the force through sickness. The survivors re-formed into coys, landed on Cuba, returned to Jamaica and as 4 volunteer coys later garrisoned Ruatan Island, Honduras Gulf. From there they surveyed the Mosquito Coast of the Gulf before being absorbed into the Jamaica Regt.

CHAPTER TWO

1 Examples of Marine actions 1755–1815.

Seven Years War 1756–63: throughout the War Mnes served in blockading ships; they were in action with Army forces in raids on the French coast and in the West Indies; other actions with the Army included the capture of Quebec (Sept '59), of Pondicherry (Jan '61), of Belle Isle (Apr–June '61), Luzon in the Phillipines (Oct '61), Port Royal Martinique (Feb '62), Havana (Aug '62); and Mnes captured Fort Louis Senegal (Apr '58) and Goree West Africa (Dec '58); actions at sea included the defeat of French ships at Quiberon Bay (Nov '59).

Operations in India 1764: with Army forces defeated nabobs before Benares surrendered (Nov).

American War of Independence 1775–83: two Mne Bns in Boston (Jan '75–Mar '76), fought at Bunker Hill; with Army in various operations including defence of Quebec (Dec '75), landings at Charlestown, South Carolina (June '76), outflanked Americans at Brandywine Creek, Pa (Sept '77), capture of Pondicherry, India (Oct '78), capture of St Lucia (Dec '78), surrendered at Yorktown, Va (Oct '81), capture of Dutch settlements in India and Ceylon (Nov '81 and Jan '82); at sea Battles of Cape St Vincent (Jan '80), of Martinique (Apr '80), of Dogger Bank (Aug '81), Battle of the Saints (Apr '82); small actions included loss of all Mnes of *Glatton* in capturing *Nymph* (Aug '80), also in *Glasgow's* 2-hour fight with American sqn (Apr '76), in *Seraphis* captured by John Paul Jones' *Bonhomme Richard* (Sept '79), all but 2 of *Monarch's* mnes were killed in action of Providien (Apr '82).

Australia 1788–91: Mne coys guarded convicts transported to Botany Bay.

French Revolutionary Wars 1793–1802: with Army at Toulon (Apr–Dec '93), capture of Martinique (Mar '94), on Corsica (Apr '94), capture of Cape Town (July '95), Mne Bn at capture of St Lucia and Grenada (May–June '96), in Acre garrison (Mar–May '99), in Holland (Aug–Oct '99), bn in Elba defences (Sept 1800), in Aboukir landings (Mar '01); also helped Maltese guerrillas (Oct '98), retook Minorca (Nov '98), occupied Madeira (July 1801); minor actions at sea included *Europa's* Mnes landed to protect French Royalists against 800 slaves at Domingo (Sept '93), in cutting out operations.

Napoleonic Wars 1803–15 and War with America 1812–15: bn at capture of Cape Town (Jan '06), of Buenos Aires (July '06) but overwhelmed here (Aug '06), captured bases in Uruguay and Montevideo (Feb '07), bn landed at Walcheren (Aug–Sept '09), capture of Reunion and Mauritios (July and Dec '10), bn in lines of Torres Vedras for a year (from Nov '10). 1st and 2nd Bns at Chesapeake Bay (Aug '13), occupied Hampton, Va (June '13), capture of Washington, DC (24 Aug 1814), only successful attack at New Orleans (Jan '15). Covered Army re-embarkation Corunna (Jan '09); raids on North Spanish coast (June–Dec '12), on American coast ('14), on Florida coast (Jan–Mar '15). At sea Mnes in cutting out operations, at Battle of Trafalgar ('05) and bombardment of Constantinople (Feb '07).

CHAPTER THREE

1 Naval Mutinies in the 1790s. In 1794 HMS *Culloden* mutinied, her crew flogging several Marines for not joining them. Other isolated mutinies occurred in the next 3 years before Apr 1797 when the fleet at Spithead and later the fleet off the Nore mutinied. Most Marines remained loyal to their

officers. In the Mediterranean Adm Lord St Vincent mounted guards with his ships' detachments 'berthing Marines close aft to the gun-room netting'.

CHAPTER FOUR

1 Examples of Marine actions 1816–1913.

1st Burma War 1823–26: landed in Rangoon and with sqn opening the river route inland up the Irrawaddy.

1st Ashanti War 1824–31: in force defending Cape Castle, 1824.

Battle of Navarino, 20 Oct 1827: 22 Mnes killed, 29 wounded.

Carlist War 1834–39: RM Bn with British Legion supporting the Queen of Spain's forces.

1st Maori War 1835–48: helped defend Russell (North Island) in Mar 1845 and at capture of Maori strongholds later.

Crimean War 1853–56: served in ships and landed with forces investing Sevastopol.

2nd Opium War 1856–60: defended British warehouses in Canton, provided garrisons for key forts and with Army forces in storming Canton, 1857, and other operations.

Operations in Japan 1863–65: RM Bn and Fleet Mnes occupied batteries at Simonoski and other landings.

2nd Ashanti War 1873–74: Mnes in force of 517 which defeated 3,000 Ashanti at Elmina.

Zulu War 1879: Active's detachment in action on the Inyezane river, other Marines in Army forces.

Operations in Egypt 1882–86: 450 Fleet Mnes landed Alexandria with 150 seamen and 60 US Mnes (July 1882) after bombardment. *Ad hoc* RM Bn of 1,000 Fleet Mnes joined by RM Bn of 559 in various actions including the 2nd Battle of Kassassin and in van of Army force at Tel-el-Kebir before reaching Cairo in Sept 1882. Fleet Mnes formed a bn at Suakin (Sudan Red Sea port) and in various actions there in 1884. Provided a coy of the Guards Camel Regt in Nov.

3rd Burma War 1885: Fleet Mnes armed river launches and with guns in barges operated on river Irrawaddy and Chindwin until several months after peace was signed.

Reconquest of Sudan 1896–98: Several RMA officers and 9 Cpls commanded Nile gunboats, other officers and NCOs were among the advisers to the Egyptian Army.

Boer War 1899–1902: 290 Fleet Mnes and 53 seamen landed; this Naval Brigade had heavy losses at the Battle of Graspan, Nov 1899. Mnes provided guards and one crew for naval guns on mobile mountings.

Boxer Rising 1900–01: 82 Mnes, 125 armed civilians and 53 US Mnes in Legation Guard of 543 in Peking during May 1900; Fleet Mnes landed with Army relief force of mainly Russians and reached Peking in Aug.

2 Robert's mountings. These enabled a mortar to be suspended almost free of the vessel's roll, for a strong horizontal bar above the mortar carried its trunion on 2 wrought iron arms which oscillated with the motion of the vessel; the muzzle was held in an iron band also linked to the arms. This kept the elevation at 42 degrees, and aim and range were altered by moving the vessel itself rather than by changing the elevation and position of the mortar.

3 Minie Rifle. A muzzle loader issued to some RMs in 1851 and sighted for ranges of up to 1,000 yds.

4 Corps' strengths. On the founding of the modern Corps in 1755 the establishment was 5,000 and subsequently varied substantially. Its peak in the 18th century was 25,300 in 1782 (War of American Independence), yet it had slumped to 3,200 by 1786. In the 19th century it reached over 30,000 during the Napoleonic Wars, but by 1900 it had fallen to 18,500. The Corps reached its highest strength in 1944 with an establishment of 78,400; at present there are under 10,000 serving Marines.

CHAPTER FIVE

1 RMA and RMLI Units of World War I and 1919.

Brigade and Battalions formed 2 Aug 1914 as RM Bde (the Flying Column) with 1 RMA Bn and 3 of RMLI (Chatham, Portsmouth and Plymouth Bns). Reorganised Sept with Deal Bn replacing the RMA Bn and recruits replacing the gunnery rates in other bns. Later redesignated 3rd Bde of RN Division and in Mar 1915 passed to Army command with RN Div. Deal Bn with 1st Bde (RN Div) Mar–Aug 1915. Major reorganisation 2 Aug 1915 as 2nd Bde with 1/RMLI Bn (men from Chatham and Deal Bns), 2/RMLI (men from Portsmouth and Plymouth Bns) and 2 seamen bns (Howe and Anson). Redesignated 1st Bde of RN Div May 1916 and 188th Bde on 16 July. On 29 Apr 1918 men of 2/RMLI absorbed by 1/RMLI which was disbanded June 1919.

3rd Bn RMLI formed 1916 for garrison duties in eastern Mediterranean; strength raised to 1,400 by Sept 1918 to include AA gunners, signallers and specialists. Disbanded in June 1921.

4th Bn RM formed 6 Feb 1918 for Zeebrugge operation from coys at Divisions preparing to go to Ireland plus 134 volunteers from the Grand Fleet; embarked strength in Apr 1918 was 723. Disbanded 27 Apr 1918.

5th Bn RM formed Sept 1918 to operate controlled coastal minefields. Disbanded Jan–Feb 1919.

6th Bn RM formed July 1919 for IS duties but instead sent to North Russia. Disbanded 15 Oct 1919.

7th Bn RM briefly formed for IS duties summer 1918.

1st Reserve Bn RMLI formed at Blandford for replacements for RMLI bns in France from June 1916–18.

Howitzer Bde RMA formed Feb–Mar 1915 with 10 specially built 15-in (381 mm) howitzers, each with a crew of 5 officers and 83 other ranks.

AA Bde RMA first battery formed Nov 1914 with 2-pdr Pom-Poms in armoured lorries and Maxim MG in motorcycle combinations. By June 1916 all btys under Army command but for a single 3-in Bty RM in Chatham AA defences. HQ returned to UK in 1915 but btys not disbanded until Feb 1919.

Other Units were: Heavy Siege train with 2 × 12-in Mark *X* guns in Belgium at first manned by seamen, but manned by 460 all ranks of RMA from Mar 1918 until disbanded in Mar 1919; RMA guns' crews with RM btys in East Africa from Feb 1916–Jan 1918; RMA gunners with South African Artillery Btys Nov 1914–Oct 1917; RM Transport Coys Oct 1914–Aug 1915; RM Div Engineers (including RM Sigs Coy) served with 3rd Bde and its successors but transferred to Royal Engineers in 1917; RM Field Ambulances formed Nov 1914–Nov 1918; RM Labour Corps operated port installations Feb 1917–early 1919; RM Engineers with a strength of about 10,000 was raised in Dec 1917 for the Admiralty's civil engineering work until Dec 1918, when only 2,000 were retained for port clearance duties until early 1919.

2 RM armoured cars. First cars used were brought to Dunkirk in August 1914 (not to be confused with civilian cars with the Flying Column). The Admiralty had purchased 100 cars or chassis for conversion into armoured cars to defend RN Air Stations. In Dec 1914 the first 3 silver Ghost Rolls Royce fully armoured cars reached Dunkirk, and similar Lanchester, Talbot and Delauney-Belville cars soon followed. Although these were all RNAS vehicles, Marines manned some or were part of the crews in others.

3 Examples of actions in World War I.

Western Europe. 1914: RM Flying Column to Ostend, 25–31 Aug; 200 Mnes with RNAS Car Sqn 12 Sept–3 Nov; RM Bde in action at Antwerp in Oct with losses of 25 killed and 416 wounded or missing. *1915:* first gun of Howitzer Bde in action 6 Mar, subsequently all 10 guns served here before Nov 1918; first bty of AA Bde in action 28 Apr. *1916:* In May 1/RMLI and 2/RMLI landed in France from Gallipoli; at battle of Ancre Heights near Beaumont Hamel (12–15 Oct) with losses over 500 all ranks. *1917:* 1/RMLI and 2/RMLI in various actions including Miraumont (17–18 Feb), 2nd Battle of the Scarpe (Apr), 2nd Battle of Passchendaele (Oct) and Welch Ridge (30 Dec). *1918:* 1/RMLI and 2/RMLI in various actions including the 1st and 2nd Battles of Bapaume (24 Mar and 2 Sept) and Battle of Cambrai (28 Sept), and advance on Mons (Nov).

Gallipoli. 1915: RM Bde mounted raids on forts in Mar with losses 22 killed and 22 wounded; Plymouth Bn landed 'Y' Beach, 23 Apr, with losses 331 killed or wounded; Chatham Bn in Anzac beachhead, 28 Apr–12 May, with losses 238 killed, 793 wounded and 122 missing; bns' other actions included the 2nd and 3rd Battles of Krithnia, 27 May and 4 June, and action at Achi Baba, 12 July, elements of RM bns in line 15 Aug–9 Jan 1916.

At sea. 1914: Heligoland Bight, 28 Aug; Battle of Coronel, 1 Nov, with losses 196 killed; Battle of Falkland Islands, 8 Dec. *1915:* Battle of Dogger Bank, 24 Jan; formations of Defensively Armed Merchant Ships' detachments, mostly RN gunners but it included 2,000 Mnes in DAMS and in some 'Q' ships. *1916:* Battle of Jutland, 31 May, with losses 538 killed and 51 wounded.

4 German strong points of 1917. Many were so well built with concrete walls that heavy guns had to be used to uproot them. One 'farmhouse' shelled by the Howitzer Bde required several 6,350kg shells to destroy the 2-metre thick reinforced-concrete walls camouflaged under laths, plaster 'bricks', etc.

5 *Vindictive* carried 16 gangways from her extra 'landing' deck, and as well as her 10 5-in guns she had: 2 flame-thrower towers (port side), bow and midship 7.5-in hows, 6 Stokes guns in boat deck bty and 6 on forecastle, 2 crews in each bty being RMA, the boat deck bty to be landed, 4 Lewis and 2 1½-pdr Pom-Poms in fighting top manned by RMA, 2 Vickers and several Lewis guns on decks.

6 RM Field Force (North Russia). Formed 5 May 1918 with 365 all ranks equipped with cold weather clothing and Westinghouse rifles. They landed in Murmansk on 31 May where HMS *Glory* had a detachment of 176 Mnes, some replacing seamen and others carrying out IS duties in the port. The Field Force operations were mainly along the Murmansk railway; in Jan–Mar 1919 they trained as ski

troops. After service on the Dwina river the Force sailed for the UK on 10 July and were disbanded there.

7 Examples of RM deployments 1920–39. *1920–37:* Mnes in sqns in China station in various actions to protect British interest on the Yangtse and other rivers. *8th RM Bn* protected Coast Guard and Signal Stations in Ireland June 1920–Spring 1922. *11th RM Bn* deployed in Constantinople with a strength of about 700 all ranks 3 Oct 1922–Aug 1923. *12th RM* Bn formed Jan 1927 for service in Shanghai, landed in China in Feb, half Bn returned to UK in Oct and remainder followed in Dec, the Bn being disbanded in Jan 1928.

CHAPTER SIX

1 Examples of actions and deployments in World War II.

Western Europe. 1940: Fleet Mnes and seamen in action Norway, Apr–May; RM Coys landed The Hague, Boulogne and Calais (with losses Calais 85 all ranks killed or captured): RM AA Btys in UK air defences at various times. *1942:* 40 Cdo landed Dieppe with heavy losses, 19 Aug; RM canoeists raid on Bordeaux, Dec. *1944:* RM Armoured Support Group in first waves of D-Day invasion on 6 June, with 41, 45, 47 and 48 Cdos landed for flank force operations and 46 Cdo landed 7 June; RM Cdos in advance to Scheldt, Aug–Sept; RM AA Bde in air defences of Scheldt and ground support fire roles, Oct 1944–Mar 1945. RM Cdos in assault on Walcheren where RM gun crews of support craft also in action, 1 Nov. *1945:* RM Cdos in Cdo Bdes' actions in the Maas river area and cruising Rhine, Weser, Aller and Elbe.

Mediterranean and Italy. 1940: RM AA Btys in defence of Malta until Jan 1942. *1941:* RM AA Btys and other units in Crete defence, May. *1942:* 11th RM Bn lose 217 men in landing repulsed at Tobruk. *1943:* 40 and 41 Cdos as flank forces landed Sicily, with 7th RM Bn in beach defences, 10 July; 7th RM Bn in crossing of Dittaino river, 19 July; RM Cdos and other units in actions in Sicily and later in Italy, the Aegean, Yugoslavia and Albania until May 1945.

Southern Asia and the Pacific. 1941: Small RM Special Service force in guerrilla landings, Malaya, Dec. *1942:* Fleet Mnes in defence of Singapore, Feb, and coast gunners formed into Force 'Viper' for river actions in Burma, Feb–Mar. *1944:* 44 Cdo in raids on Arakan coast, Mar; 42 Cdo in line and island raids, Arakan, Nov. *1945:* RM Cdos in 3 Cdo Bde's landings at Myebon and Kangaw, Jan–Feb; Fleet Mnes landed unopposed Cheduba Island, Jan; RM canoeists in coast raids and recces, Feb–July.

Actions at sea. 1940–45: RM detachments served in battleships and cruisers throughout the war.

CHAPTER SEVEN

1 Examples of operations and deployments by land and sea 1946–80.

NATO territories, Africa and Middle East. 1946: RM personnel in Rhine Flotilla (Germany) which became RM commitment in the 1950s and early 1960s. *1948:* 40 Cdo (hereafter '40') protect docks at Haifa, Palestine in Jan. '42' as UN protection force in Tripoli and '45' same duties at Benghazi, Libya, Feb; '42' security duties in Jerusalem Apr; '45' security duties Haifa before returning to Benghazi, May; '42' briefly in Haifa and '45' covered withdrawal of last British presence in Palestine, June; '42' to Canal Zone, Egypt for internal security (IS) duties until Mar 1949; '40' to Cyprus for IS duties, 1 Nov 1948–Mar 1949. *1953:* '40' to Canal Zone, Egypt for IS duties, Feb; '42', '45' and Bde HQ to Canal Zone for IS duties, May. *1954:* 3 Cdo Bde form strategic reserve in Malta, Aug 1954–Oct 1956. *1955:* 3 Cdo Bde HQ, '40' and '45' in anti-terrorist ops in Cyprus, 10 Sept 1955–Aug 1956. *1956:* 3 Cdo Bde, '40' and '45' joined by '42' from UK prepare for ops in Egypt, Aug–Oct; '40', '42', '45' and Cdo Bde Hq landed to seize Port Said, Egypt before main Army forces landed, 6–14 Nov; RM Coy to guard naval base Londonderry, Northern Ireland, Dec. *1957:* '40' in Cyprus for tours of anti-terrorist ops, Feb 1957–Apr 1959; '45' joined '40' in Cyprus for tours, May 1957–Dec 1958. *1959:* '45' Cdo begin 7 years of operations in Aden, 4 Apr. *1961:* '40' form Malta garrison, Apr; '42' and '45' in Kuwait, July; '43' provide guards for Bermuda conference, Dec. *1964:* '41' as first Cdo as UK Spearhead Bn, 4 Jan; '45' to Tanganyika and '41' to Kenya before relieving '45'; '43' in major exercise in N Africa. (Only examples of the many exercises are given in this note.) *1965:* '43' in first full Cdo exercise in Norway, 20 Mar. *1967:* '42' joined '45' in Aden where '42' was the last British force to withdraw on 28–29 Nov. *1969:* '45' in Cdo ship with NATO forces in Mediterranean, Sept; '41' to Northern Ireland in first of RM Cdos' 4-month tours in the present emergency, 28 Sept (from this date one or more Cdos deployed there in turn with Army Bns throughout 1970s). *1972:* 3 Cdo Bde began continuing commitment to NATO's northern flank in Allied Forces North Command, Jan; Cdos in operation 'Motorman' in Northern Ireland, June; '42' in first Cdo exercise in Canada, Oct. *1973:* Cdo exercises in N Norway involved an increasing number of Cdo units and took on the pattern of exercises which continues in the 1980s. *1974:* '41' in Canada, June; '40' from UK and '41' from Cdo ship to Cyprus, 17 July–16 Sept; '41' with UN Forces in Cyprus, Nov 1974–Apr 1975; Navl Party 8901 of RM cdos continued to garrison Falkland Islands. *1978:* Cdos in major NATO exercise in N Norway, Mar; first 10-man detachments joined frigates, Nov. *1979:* first full deployment of 3 Cdo Bde in Norwegian exercises, Jan–Mar; Salerno Coy RM last British garrison withdrawn from Malta, 30 Mar; RM detachment in Commonwealth forces in Rhodesia-Zimbabwe, Dec. *1980:* 3 Cdo in Norway on exercises with Norwegian, Dutch and USMC forces, Jan–Mar; '45' on exercises in Sardinia, May.

Far East. 1946: '40' and '42' in 3 Cdo Bde as military administration Hong Kong. *1949:* 3 Cdo Bde on IS duties in Hong Kong, Aug 1949–May 1950. *1950:* 3 Cdo Bde of '40', '42' and '45' first deployed in anti-terrorist ops in Malaya, summer 1950–Mar 1952; 41 (Independent) Cdo RM to Korea where in ops including Chosin retreat (Dec 1950) and island raids, etc until withdrawn in Feb 1952. *1951:* 3 Cdo Bde on IS duties in Malaya. *1956:* LC crews in back-up for atom bomb test on Christmas Island, summer. *1960:* '42' in Cdo ship based in Singapore, May. *1962:* '40' and '42' in Borneo ops including rescue of British official at Limbang in opening phase of Indonesian confrontation. *1963:* '40' and '42' in tours of Borneo until late 1966. *1967:* '40' in IS duties Hong Kong, May; 3 Cdo Bde with '40' and '45' based Singapore, May. *1971:* '40' with USMC in Philippines exercises, Apr. *1979:* '42' with Raiding Sqn to prevent illegal immigration into Hong Kong, Sept–Oct *1980:* Raiding Sqn personnel (later as 3 Raiding Sqn) continued in Hong Kong; M Coy '42' on IS duties in New Hebrides, June.

Bibliography

Histories and Memoirs
Aiken, Alex, *In Time of War*, Glasgow 1980
Anderson, M. S., *The Ascendancy of Europe 1815–1914*, London 1972
Blumberg, H. E., *Britain's Sea Soldiers: a record of the Royal Marines during 1914–1919*, Devonport 1927
Bush, E., *Gallipoli*, London 1973
Carswell, J., *From Revolution to Revolution*, London 1973
Clowes, W. L., *The Royal Navy: a history Vols I–VII*, London 1899
Edye, L., *History of the Royal Marine Forces 1664–1701*, London 1893
Field, C., *Britain's Sea Soldiers Vols I and II*, Liverpool 1924
Gilbert, John, *Discovery and Exploitation: Charting the Vast Pacific*, London 1979
Hart, Liddell, *A History of the World War 1914–1918*, London 1930
Hampshire, Cecil, *The Royal Marines Tercentenary 1664–1964*, privately published London 1964
Healis, R., *Adventure Glorious*, London 1955
Jones, J. R., *The Restored Monarchy*, London 1979
Judd, D., *The Crimean War*, London 1975

Ladd, J. D., *Commandos and Rangers of World War II*, London 1978
Ladd, J. D., *The Royal Marines 1919–1980*, London 1980
Moulton, J. L., *The Royal Marines*, London 1972
Nicolas, P. H., *Royal Marines Forces Vols I and II*, London 1840
Pemberton, W. B., *Battles of the Crimea*, London 1975
Read, J., *The War in the Peninsula*, London 1977
Terraine, J., *Trafalgar*, London 1976
Times History of the War in South Africa Vols II and III, London 1905
Warner, O., *Trafalgar*, London 1959
Warner, P., *The Zeebrugge Raid*, London 1978

Articles and references
Blumberg, H. E., *A Record of the Royal Marines Vols I–III*, extracts published by RM Historical Society, Portsmouth 1980
Boatner, M. M., *Biographical Dictionary of American War of Independence 1763–93*, London 1973
Davy Navy Records Society, *Queen Anne's Navy*, London 1961
Davy Navy Records Society, *The Manning of the Royal Navy*, London 1976
Dictionary of American History, New York 1940
Fabb, J., *The Uniforms of Trafalgar*, London 1977
Globe and Laurel, the journal of the Royal Marines
Pemsel, H., *Atlas of Naval Warfare*, London 1975

Acknowledgements

Photographs

Bodleian Library, Oxford 12; Castle Museum, Nottingham 41; Central Office of Information, London 132–133, 141; City Art Gallery, Bristol 47; Commando News Team 151 top, 152; Richard Cooke, London 3–4, 162 top, 162–163 top, 162–163 bottom, 163 bottom, 166–167; Director of Public Relations (RN) 136 top; 40 Commando News Team, 155 bottom; HMS Excellent 97 bottom left; HMS Intrepid 150 bottom; Hamlyn Group Picture Library 42, 62–63, 72 top, 72 bottom, 75 bottom, 110–111; Major A. J. Hawley 130 bottom; Imperial War Museum, London 53, 60, 67 bottom, 81, 84–85, 101, 102, 104 top, 104 bottom, 105, 106 bottom, 107, 113, 115; Ministry of Defence, London 163 top; Mitchell Library, Sydney 39; National Army Museum, London 64 top; National Maritime Museum, London 13, 14–15, 22, 24–25, 26–27, 36, 45, 56–57, 64 bottom, 103; Peabody Museum, Salem, Massachusetts 54; Provincial Archives, Victoria, British Columbia 67 top; RM Museum, Eastney 11, 25, 28, 33, 37, 40, 61, 66, 68 top, 68 centre, 68 bottom, 69 top, 69 bottom, 70–71, 73 top, 73 bottom, 74, 76, 77, 78 top left, 78 bottom left, 79 top right, 79 bottom right, 80 top, 80 bottom, 82–83, 86–87, 89 top, 89 bottom, 90, 94–95, 97 top left, 97 top right, 97 bottom right, 98 top left, 98 top right, 98 bottom, 100, 106 top, 114, 116 top, 116 bottom, 117, 118, 120–121, 122, 124–125, 126, 130 top, 131 top, 131 bottom, 134–135, 136 bottom, 137 top, 138–139, 143, 150 top, 151 bottom, 154, 155 top, 156 top, 156 bottom, 158 top, 158 bottom, 158–159, 159 top, 159 bottom, 160 top, 160 bottom, 161, 164, 165; RM Museum – Photo Precision 18–19; RM Museum – Public Record Office 9; RM Official Photographs 126–127, 137 bottom, 140, 142, 157 top, 157 bottom; RN Official Photograph 148; The Star, Johannesburg, Barnett Collection 75 top; US Marine Corps 129 top, US Navy 129 bottom.

Index